1991–1993 Examin
Suggested Solutions

Company Law

LLB

University of London
External Examinations

HLT Publications

HLT PUBLICATIONS
200 Greyhound Road, London W14 9RY

Examination Questions
© The University of London 1991, 1992, 1993
Solutions © The HLT Group Ltd 1994

All HLT publications enjoy copyright protection and the copyright belongs to The HLT Group Ltd.

All rights reserved. No part of this publication may be reproduced or transmitted in any form or by any means, electronic, mechanical, photocopying, recording or otherwise, or stored in any retrieval system of any nature without either the written permission of the copyright holder, application for which should be made to The HLT Group Ltd, or a licence permitting restricted copying in the United Kingdom issued by the Copyright Licensing Agency.

Any person who infringes the above in relation to this publication may be liable to criminal prosecution and civil claims for damages.

ISBN 0 7510 0418 9

British Library Cataloguing-in-Publication.

A CIP Catalogue record for this book is available from the British Library.

Printed and bound in Great Britain.

CONTENTS

Acknowledgement   page v

Introduction   vii

Questions and Suggested Solutions

    1991   1

    1992   29

    1993   61

ACKNOWLEDGEMENT

The questions used are taken from past University of London LLB (External) Degree examination papers and our thanks are extended to the University of London for the kind permission which has been given to us to use and publish the questions.

Caveat:

The answers given are not approved or sanctioned by the University of London and are entirely our responsibility.

They are not intended as 'Model Answers', but rather as Suggested Solutions.

The answers have two fundamental purposes, namely:

1. To provide a detailed example of a suggested solution to examination questions, and

2. To assist students with their research into the subject and to further their understanding and appreciation of the subject of Laws.

Note:

Please note that the solutions in this book were written in the year of the examination for each paper. They were appropriate solutions at the time of preparation, but students must note that certain caselaw and statutes may subsequently have changed.

INTRODUCTION

Why choose HLT publications

Holborn College has earned an International reputation over the past ten years for the outstanding quality of its teaching, Textbooks, Casebooks and Suggested Solutions to past examination papers set by the various examining bodies.

Our expertise is reflected in the outstanding results achieved by our students in the examinations conducted by the University of London, the Law Society, the Council of Legal Education and the Associated Examining Board.

The object of Suggested Solutions

The Suggested Solutions have been prepared by College lecturers experienced in teaching to this specific syllabus and are intended to be an example of a full answer to the problems posed by the examiner.

They are not 'model answers', for at this level there almost certainly is not just one answer to a problem, nor are the answers written to strict examination time limits.

The opportunity has been taken, where appropriate, to develop themes, suggest alternatives and set out additional material to an extent not possible by the examinee in the examination room.

We feel that in writing full opinion answers to the questions that we can assist you with your research into the subject and can further your understanding and appreciation of the law.

Notes on examination technique

Although the SUBSTANCE and SLANT of the answer changes according to the subject-matter of the question, the examining body and syllabus concerned, the TECHNIQUE of answering examination questions does not change.

You will not pass an examination if you do not know the substance of a course. You may pass if you do not know how to go about answering a question although this is doubtful. To do well and to guarantee success, however, it is necessary to learn the technique of answering problems properly. The following is a guide to acquiring that technique.

Time

All examinations permit only a limited time for papers to be completed. All papers require you to answer a certain number of questions in that time, and the questions, with some exceptions carry equal marks.

It follows from this that you should never spend a disproportionate amount of time on any question. When you have used up the amount of time allowed for any one question STOP and go on to the next question after an abrupt conclusion, if necessary. If you feel that you are running out of time, then complete your answer in note form. A useful way of ensuring that you do not over-run is to write down on a piece of scrap paper the time at which you should be starting each part of the paper. This can be done in the few minutes before the examination begins and it will help you to calm any nerves you may have.

Reading the question

It will not be often that you will be able to answer every question on an examination paper. Inevitably, there will be some areas in which you feel better prepared than others. You will prefer to answer the questions which deal with those areas, but you will never know how good the questions are unless you read the whole examination paper.

You should spend at least 10 MINUTES at the beginning of the examination reading the questions. Preferably, you should read them more than once. As you go through each question, make a brief note on the examination paper of any relevant cases and/or statutes that occur to you even if you think you may not answer that question: you may well be grateful for this note towards the end of the examination when you are tired and your memory begins to fail.

Re-reading the answers

Ideally, you should allow time to re-read your answers. This is rarely a pleasant process, but will ensure that you do not make any silly mistakes such as leaving out a 'not' when the negative is vital.

The structure of the answer

Almost all examination problems raise more than one legal issue that you are required to deal with. Your answer should include the following:

Identify the issues raised by the question

This is of crucial importance and gives shape to the whole answer. It indicates to the examiner that you appreciate what he is asking you about.

This is at least as important as actually answering the questions of law raised by that issue.

The issues should be identified in the first paragraph of the answer.

Deal with those issues one by one as they arise in the course of the problem

This, of course, is the substance of the answer and where study and revision pays off.

If the answer to an issue turns on a provision of a statute, CITE that provision briefly, but do not quote it from any statute you may be permitted to bring into the examination hall.

Having cited the provision, show how it is relevant to the question.

If there is no statute, or the meaning of the statute has been interpreted by the courts, CITE the relevant cases

'Citing cases' does not mean writing down the nature of every case that happens to deal with the general topic with which you are concerned and then detailing all the facts you can think of.

You should cite only the most relevant cases – there may perhaps only be one. No more facts should be stated than are absolutely essential to establish the relevance of the case. If there is a relevant case, but you cannot remember its name, it is sufficient to refer to it as 'one decided case'.

Whenever a statute or case is cited, the title of statute or the name of the case should be underlined

This makes the examiner's job much easier because he can see at a glance whether the relevant material has been dealt with, and it will make him more disposed in your favour.

Having dealt with the relevant issues, summarise your conclusions in such a way that you answer the question

A question will often say at the end simply 'Advise A', or B, or C, etc. The advice will usually turn on the individual answers to a number of issues. The point made here is that the final paragraph should pull those individual answers together and actually give the advice required. For example, it may begin something like: 'The effect of the answer to the issues raised by this question is that one's advice to A is that ...'

Related to the previous paragraph, make sure at the end that you have answered the question

For example, if the question says 'Advise A', make sure that is what your answer does. If you are required to advise more than one party, make sure that you have dealt with all the parties that you are required to and no more.

Some general points

You should always try to get the examiner on your side. One method has already been mentioned – the underlining of case names, etc. There are also other ways as well.

Always write as neatly as you can. This is more easily done with ink than with a ball-point.

Avoid the use of violently coloured ink eg turquoise; this makes a paper difficult to read.

Space out your answers sensibly: leave a line between paragraphs. You can always get more paper. At the same time, try not to use so much paper that your answer book looks too formidable to mark. This is a question of personal judgment.

NEVER put in irrelevant material simply to show that you are clever. Irrelevance is not a virtue and time spent on it is time lost for other, relevant, answers.

UNIVERSITY OF LONDON
LLB EXAMINATION 1991
PART II for External Students

COMPANY LAW

Tuesday, 4 June: 2.30 pm to 5.30 pm

Answer *FOUR* questions, including at least ONE from Section A and at least TWO from Section B.

SECTION A

1 'The rule in *Salomon v Salomon & Co Ltd* has been successfully avoided where it is to the benefit of the shareholders and directors for it to be so avoided. Where, however, the issue is whether the directors or shareholders should be liable for the company's debts, the courts have been very reluctant to bypass the rule. It has been left largely to the legislature to act in this regard.'
   Discuss.

2 'The common law was unable to solve the problems created where negotiations conducted prior to the incorporation of a company were intended to result in a contract binding on that company when incorporated. The legislature eventually had to step in.'
   What were these problems? Do you agree that the common law did not offer a satisfactory solution? Has the legislature now solved these problems satisfactorily?

3 'The regime of Administration was introduced on the recommendations of the Cork Committee to enable an insolvent company with the potential for partial or total recovery to avoid the destructive effects of liquidation.'
   Assess the effectiveness of the means by which the legislation empowers the regime of Administration to achieve this end. To the extent that you believe that the regime fails in its purpose, what changes would you recommend?

SECTION B

4 Jumbo Limited ('the company') was formed to run the business formerly carried on in partnership by Arthur, Basil, and Charles, each of whom was appointed as a director of the company. Each owns 100 of the 300 issued shares. The articles of association of the company contain, among other provisions, the following regulations:

> '28A Where any shareholder wishes to transfer his shares, he shall offer them for sale to the other shareholders who shall purchase them at an agreed or an arbitrated price.
>
> 80A A resolution for the dismissal of any director of the company will not be passed unless Arthur votes in favour of such resolution.'

After a number of years, a difference of opinion grew up between Arthur, on the one hand, and Basil and Charles on the other. The latter wished to expand the company's business, but Arthur was opposed to their plans.

The assets of the company were recently valued at £3m and Arthur has called on Basil and Charles to purchase his shares for £1m. They have refused and have proposed a resolution for the dismissal of Arthur from the board of directors of the company.

Discuss.

5 Henry is the majority shareholder and managing director of Bat and Ball Ltd ('the company'), whose business consists of selling sports equipment. Owing to the recession, Henry lent the company £50,000 on 1 January 1989, but by the middle of 1989 business had hardly improved and Henry, worried about his loan, caused the company to grant him a fixed charge over its shop and book debts as security for a further loan of £50,000. In November 1989 the Midwest bank, where the company's overdraft was £75,000, threatened to petition for the winding up of the company unless it was given some form of security. As a result, Henry caused the company to grant a floating charge to the bank over all the company's assets.

Although the position looked increasingly hopeless, Henry, on the advice of his accountant, continued trading because an end to the recession was widely forecast. In fact, this turned out to be too optimistic a forecast and in November 1990, a petition was presented for the winding up of the company and a winding up order was granted in March 1991. For the six months prior to the grant of the winding up order, Henry only drew half his agreed salary (ie £1,500 per month instead of £3,000).

The company's fixed assets and book debts are valued at £50,000 and the company's other assets would yield £10,000.

Advise the liquidator.

6 The main business of Elite Properties plc is the acquisition, development, and disposition of property. There are 8 directors who own 15m of the company's 25m issued £1 shares. At a meeting of the board of directors about a year ago, a proposal was presented for the purchase of a site adjoining a rubbish dump. Although the price asked was low (£3m for 7 acres), it was felt that the situation might make it difficult to develop the site and sell any houses.

The site in question was, in fact, bought by Speculative Enterprises Ltd, whose share capital is held as to 25% by Donald, Edward and Fred all of whom are directors of Elite Properties. Speculative Enterprises paid £2.5m for the site and a few weeks later sold it for £5m.

At a shareholders' meeting of Elite Properties called to discuss the failure by Elite to purchase the site, the directors used their votes to prevent the passing of a resolution (a) calling on the directors to compensate the company for any loss caused by the failure to purchase the site and (b) calling on Donald, Edward and Fred to account for all profit made as shareholders and directors of Speculative Enterprises Ltd.

Discuss.

7 The objects clause of Mainstream Ltd ('the company') states:

'The purpose of the company is the manufacture and distribution of reading material for children under the age of 7.'

The articles of association restrict any borrowing by the company except by resolution of the directors. In fact, for the past few years, only Keith of the three person board was active in the running of the company. Lorna and Mary who had started the company with Keith were now spending most of their time with their young children and it was understood that Keith would carry on the day to day management of the company.

Last year Keith after discussions with the company's bank manager, arranged for the borrowing of £50,000 and used it to purchase a major shareholding in a publishing company (Highlight Ltd) which concentrates on publishing pornographic literature and of which Keith is a director. Owing to recent legislation placing severe restraints on the publishing of pornography, the company's shares in Highlight are now virtually worthless.

Discuss.

8   The share capital of Rain and Sun Ltd ('the company') consists of 80,000 £1 ordinary shares which are owned by Alan and Benjamin equally. There are also 20,000 £1 9% cumulative preference shares owned as to 7,500 each by Alan and Benjamin and 5,000 by Carol. The preference shares are participating as to dividends and have priority in repayment on a winding up. There is also a provision in the company articles to the effect that any shareholder with 5% or more of the share capital may veto any variation of the company's capital structure.

Alan and Benjamin are now proposing to reduce the capital of the company by repaying the preference shareholders in full and eliminating the preference shares. Although the company has made large profits over the past three years, no dividends have been declared.

Not surprisingly, Carol is wholly opposed to this proposal. Advise her.

PART A
QUESTION 1

General Comment

The concept of corporate personality has been proving to be a popular topic over a number of years. The basic thrust of the question is whether legislation has proved more effective in lifting the veil of incorporation compared to the role played by the courts in this area.

Skeleton Solution

Principle of corporate personality ie: no personal liability – state exceptions – fraud, agency, unlawful purpose, trusts, taxation – legislation, s24 CA 1985 and ss213 and 214 IA 1986 – no coherent principles – veil is lifted where justice demands it – where no previous constraints of binding authority exist.

Suggested Solution

The most important consequence of incorporation is that a company becomes a legal person distinct from its members. In *Salomon* v *Salomon & Co* (1), a sole trader transferred his business to a company of which he was a sole owner and part of the purchase price was outstanding as a secured debt in the form of a debenture. The case was important because it established the legality of a 'one-man' company and the concept of separate legal entity of a company. But it also caused concern because it was possible to limit liability not merely to the money put into the company, but to avoid serious risks to some of that money by subscribing for debentures rather than shares. The decision was criticised for this reason.

The courts have continued to play an active role at times lifting the veil of incorporation and at times treating the members of the company as one and the same. It would be wrong to say that legislature played a more active role, nevertheless there are some relevant statutory provisions related to this area.

The fact that a company is a separate legal entity from its members is not necessarily wholly beneficial to those members. In

Macaura v *Northern Assurance Co Ltd* (2), as a consequence of incorporation a sole owner had no insurable interests in the assets of a company which were treated as the property of the company alone. This was also illustrated in the case of *Henry Brown* v *Smith* (3). However, a more modern example of the application of this principle is *Lee* v *Lee's Air Farming Limited* (4), where a sole owner was both director and controlling shareholder and sole employee of the company, and the court refused to lift the veil. It should also be noted that the rule in *Foss* v *Harbottle* (5) provides, subject to limited exceptions, that the proper plaintiff in respect of a breach by the director of their fiduciary duty to the company is the company itself, even where this wrongdoing had caused loss to individual shareholders.

Nevertheless, there have been several departures from this rule in order to discover why the members are shielding behind the veil of incorporation. In *Gilford Motor Company* v *Horne* (6) the distinction between the company and its members was used to evade legal obligations. In *Wallersteiner* v *Moir* (7) a series of sham companies were set up for fraudulent purposes. In *Re Bugle Press* (8) where majority shareholders set up a company to force the minority shareholder to sell out, this was held to be a sham. In fact Harman LJ went on to say that 'the minority shareholder ... has only to shout and the walls of Jericho fall flat.' On the question of agency, in appropriate circumstances, even though the company is a separate legal entity, the courts may treat the company as an agent of its shareholders as in *Smith, Stone & Knight* v *Birmingham Corporation* (9) and in *Firestone Tyre* v *Llewellin* (10), where the veil was lifted to the company's disadvantage, as it was liable to pay tax. Further, in *Trebanog Working Men's Club* v *MacDonald* (11) the principle of trusteeship was used by the courts to escape from the principle of a separate legal entity.

The most significant inroads to the concept of separate corporate personality have concerned holding and subsidiary companies. In several cases the courts have recognised the fact that a holding company and its subsidiary are often a single commercial enterprise. In *DHN Food Distributors* v *Tower Hamlets LBC* (12) a holding company was entitled to compensation on the acquisition of land held by its wholly owned subsidiary. The Cork Committee on Insolvency Law and Practice in its report, published in June 1982, stated that this area needed the widest possible review with a need to introduce reforming legislation. The committee unfortunately did not propose a solution although in certain countries, eg New Zealand, the court may hold a 'related company' liable for the debts of a failed company if it is 'just and equitable' to do so. There is, however, some evidence to suggest that the courts may be less willing to do this where the subsidiary is not wholly owned: *Multinational Gas and Petroleum Co v Multinational Gas Services Limited* (13).

As far as legislation is concerned the more important provisions under the Companies Act 1985 include s24, where personal liability is incurred if membership falls below two for more than six months; however this can be easily avoided by the transfer of one share to a nominee during the six month period and therefore s24 is of little practical importance. Directors may be liable for a third parties loss where a public company has traded without a s117 certificate under the Companies Act. By s349 Companies Act 1985 a person can be held personally liable if the company's name is not used correctly. Furthermore, the Insolvency Act 1986 namely ss213 and 214 have a more practical application where directors will be held personally liable for fraudulent or wrongful trading. However, s214 which deals with wrongful trading is a more useful provision as its ambit is wider.

Therefore in conclusion one can say that the development of the concept of lifting the veil of incorporation has been rather haphazard and irrational. The courts' policy is to lift the veil of incorporation where they think justice demands it and where they are not constrained by earlier binding authority. It is doubtful therefore whether legislation could improve the position in this area which calls, above all else, upon judicial discretion.

References

(1) [1897] AC 22
(2) [1925] AC 619
(3) [1961] Ch 270
(4) [1961] AC 12
(5) (1843) 2 Hare 461
(6) [1933] Ch 935
(7) [1974] 1 WLR 991
(8) [1961] Ch 270
(9) [1939] 4 All ER 116
(10) [1957] 1 WLR 464
(11) [1940] 1 KB 576
(12) [1976] 1 WLR 852
(13) [1983] Ch 258

QUESTION 2

General Comment

Normally a question on pre-incorporation contracts appears in a problem question; however the trust of this essay question is on the problems of pre-incorporation contracts, namely the logical impossibility of entering into such contracts, as the company at this point does not exist. Case law in this area needs consideration and the implication of s36 CA 1985 and whether this provision adequately resolves all problems in this area.

Skeleton Solution

Pre 1985 position – consideration of case law where contract would be binding depended on the words used when the contract was signed – were common law remedies adequate? – post s36(4) CA 1985 where promoters held personally liable unless contrary intention can be shown – further company may ratify original contract – conclusion, has legislation solved all problems?

Suggested Solution

Until a company is incorporated it cannot contract or enter into an agreement and in turn cannot be liable or entitled under such a contract because it is not in existence. The question whether the company was liable depended on the way in which the contract was signed. If signed 'for and on behalf of the company', then this was equated to the principle of agency and was not valid as there can be no agency whilst the principal (ie, the company) is not in existence: *Kelner* v *Baxter* (1).

Section 36C Companies Act 1985 (previously s36(4)) has clarified the position to an extent, where a promoter who enters into a pre-incorporation will be bound as principal and deemed to be personally liable by it (subject to any agreement to the contrary). This is by far the most important provision relating to pre-incorporation contracts, but there are other relevant statutory provisions. Under Companies Act 1985 s67, the primary responsibility for the accuracy of a company's prospectus rests with the directors and they will be liable to pay compensation to all persons who subscribe for shares for any loss or damage resulting from a misleading statement. Such a claim can be brought against any director or promoter or anyone who was a party to this. Moreover, s150 Financial Services Act 1986 provides a remedy to an investor who acquires securities or an interest in them and suffers loss by reason of misleading information in listing particulars.

In the past there was some doubt as to the position of a person who signs not as an agent but merely as purporting to authenticate the signature of the company. At common law this is most unlikely to place personal liability on the signer: *Newborne* v *Sensolid* (2). However, s36(4) abolishes the distinction between signature as an agent and a signature authenticating the signature of the company. Lord Denning has gone so far to say that 'this distinction has now been obliterated.' In *Phonogram Ltd* v *Lane* (3), the fact that the promoter signed 'for and on behalf' of the company made no difference to his liability. The Court of Appeal held these words were not sufficient to constitute 'an agreement to the contrary' for the purposes of s36(4) and the promoter was held personally liable as the company could not later ratify a contract made prior to its incorporation.

Therefore the only way in which the company can take over the liability is by making an entirely new contract with the third party on the same terms as that made by the promoter. The company may make such a contract either expressly or impliedly, by its conduct. To be sufficient to create a contract in these circumstances however, the company's conduct must unequivocally refer to the alleged agreement and will, even then, only amount to an offer which will be converted into a contract if the third party accepts it. This was illustrated in *Natal Land and Colonisation Co* v *Pauline Colliery & Development Syndicate* (4). The problem for the other party is to prove that the company did make a new contract after incorporation and the general attitude of the courts seems to be to require clear evidence; simply acting in the mistaken belief that a pre-incorporation contract is binding is not enough: *Re Northumberland Avenue Hotel Co* (5). However, if a company after incorporation takes possession of property transferred to it in a pre-incorporation contract, the courts may be able to infer that the only possible explanation is that a new contract was made after incorporation: *Re Patent Ivory Manufacturing Co* (6), where the directors renegotiated the terms of the pre-incorporation and this was held to amount to an offer to enter into a fresh agreement and was therefore binding on the company and the third party.

A promoter may be able to protect himself from personal liability for pre-incorporation contracts in various ways. Firstly, by making the agreement with a third party 'subject to contract'. This means that there is no contract and therefore no liability on the promoter, until the company, after incorporation, enters into the contract with the third party. Secondly, the promoter can also make the contract himself and then once the company has been incorporated, assign the benefits of the contract to it, and in return, persuade the company and the third party to enter into a contract of novation whereby the liabilities will also be transferred. However, it is difficult to imagine circumstances where a third party would agree to a non-liability clause given that such an agreement does not serve to make the company liable.

Although s36(4) is welcomed, it does not redress the problems on pre-incorporation contracts sufficiently. Perhaps this point would be of much less importance if companies could simply ratify pre-incorporation contracts, and a further statutory amendment to this effect may serve to make the law more tenable in this area.

References
(1) (1866) LR 2 CP 174
(2) [1954] 1 QB 45
(3) [1982] QB 938
(4) [1904] AC 120
(5) (1886) 33 Ch D 16
(6) (1888) 38 Ch D 156

QUESTION 3

General Comment
Question deals with the concept of corporate rescue due to changes introduced by the Insolvency Act 1986. A general review of this new system of administration orders should be made and reference has to be made to previous law. There is however little authority and case law in this area and it is necessary therefore to concentrate on statutory provisions.

Skeleton Solution
Provisions under Insolvency Act 1986 force a company to consider insolvency earlier in order to try and rescue the company and keep it as a going concern. The role of the administrator to try and achieve this – application made by company, director or creditor – other proceedings stayed to allow administrator to make proposals – procedure relatively untested, success dependent on goodwill of creditors and chargees.

Suggested Solution
Administration is a new procedure recommended by the Cork Report *The Report of the Review Committee on Insolvency and Practice 1982*. It was introduced as an alternative to receivership. The basic purpose of an administrative order is to freeze the debts of the company in financial difficulty in order to assist an administrator to save the company or at least achieve a better realisation of its assets. It is not a procedure designed for creditors to try to enforce their security. In *Re Consumer and Industrial Press Ltd* (1), Peter Gibson J said that the court had to be satisfied that it was more probable than not that one of the specified purposes would be achieved. This test was adopted in *Re Manlon Trading Ltd* (2), where on balance the courts refused to make an administration order.

The new Act therefore forces directors to assess the company's financial situation much earlier in order to benefit from this form of corporate rescue, as it may bring about a more satisfactory result for members and creditors alike. The Insolvency Act 1986 also introduced other provisions to ensure that directors do assess the company's financial position in good time under ss213 and 214 IA

1986, which deals with fraudulent and wrongful trading and imposes personal liability on directors contravening these provisions. Moreover, the Company Directors Disqualification Act 1986 provides further statutory provisions for mandatory disqualification of directors by the courts if these provisions are contravened.

A receiver on the other hand will take a charge over all the company's assets and will concentrate on paying off the company's debts, firstly to preferential creditors and he is not under a duty to rescue the company, whereas an administrator will try to salvage the company's business as a going concern.

Before making an order the court must be satisfied that the company is unlikely to be able to pay its debts and such an order will be likely to achieve the survival of the whole or part of the business as a going concern, as this order would provide a more advantageous realisation of the assets than would be effected on a winding up order. The other possible purpose for an order would be the approving of a voluntary arrangement under Part 1 of the Insolvency Act or sanctioning of a compromise or arrangement under Companies Act s425.

If satisfied that a realisation can be achieved the court will grant the order under IA 1986 s123. The company, directors or creditors can make an application for such an order under IA 1986 s9. Notice of this petition must be given to any person entitled to appoint a receiver as he must consent to such an order. The effect of the application is that the company cannot be wound up, no charge, hire purchase or retention of title clauses can be enforced against the company, without consent of the court and this also applies to any proceedings commenced against the company.

The making of such an order will automatically dismiss any outstanding winding up petition and any existing administrative receiver will have to vacate his office.

The administrator must be a qualified insolvency practitioner and his powers include management of the affairs, property and business of the company. He can deal with charged property, remove directors and require information from the officers and employees of the company, and, in exercising his powers, the administrator is deemed to be an agent of the company.

Within three months of the order, he must send to the registrar, the creditors and members a statement of his proposals for achieving the purpose of the administration. A meeting of creditors is then convened to approve these proposals: s23 IA 1986.

This meeting is an important feature of administration, as these proposals must be approved before implementation: *Re Consumer and Industrial Press Ltd (No 2)* (3). However, this committee is much weaker than the committee of creditors in a liquidation, since it has no powers to give directions to administrators, and its consent is not necessary in his discharging his duties as administrator.

However, where there is a receiver in place, the person who appointed the receiver must consent to the appointment of the administrator. This is the main failing of corporate rescue as any creditor or member may apply to the court for an order that the company is or has been managed by the administrator in a manner unfairly prejudicial to him, and the court can then make any order it thinks fit: s27 IA 1986. This provision is very similar to s459 CA 1985, and unsatisfied creditors have the opportunity to veto the appointment of an administrator.

The Cork Committee made its recommendations after studying various procedures in a number of countries including France, Australia and United States. Its observations were twofold. Firstly, whether administration will work depends on the goodwill of chargees as they can block the procedure by appointing a receiver and then vetoing the appointment of the administrator. This is because it takes a long time between applying for an order and obtaining it and this leaves time for chargees to appoint a receiver. Secondly, when a company is in financial difficulties and an administrator is appointed, the company's business may continue to suffer in that people may be reluctant to trade with the company, as they will be worried that the company may not be able to meet its financial obligations.

Therefore, although the administrator's role is geared towards rescuing a company, his task can be hindered, and his success is very much dependent on the goodwill of chargees.

References

(1) [1988] BCLC 177
(2) (1988) The Times 14 June
(3) (1987) 4 BCC 72

PART B
QUESTION 4

General Comment
The question deals with a number of areas, the rules on transfer of shares and pre-emption rights, as well as minority protection under Companies Act 1985, s459 and s122 of the Insolvency Act 1986. The issue of removing Arthur where under the articles he has enhanced voting rights, there is a need to consider *Bushell* v *Faith* (1), and if this clause can be changed under s9 CA 1985.

Skeleton Solution
Company is a quasi-partnership, therefore members must deal fairly with each other. Arthur may petition under CA 1985 s459 for his shares to be bought at a proper value or he may also petition for a winding up order under s122 Insolvency Act 1986, but this is a drastic measure – courts reluctant to wind up a running and viable business. Basil and Charles may wish to change the clause giving Arthur weighted voting rights but such a change must be bona fide for the benefit of the company.

Suggested Solution
Arthur, Basil and Charles have formed a company from what was previously a partnership. Prima facie the company has the characteristics of a quasi-partnership and in *Ebrahimi* v *Westbourne Galleries* (2) Lord Wilberforce explained 'that such partnerships were formed on the basis of a personal relationship between the participants, and that there is an understanding that each of the participants will be concerned in the management of the business.' Where the relationship of trust has broken down, as seems to be the case here, it may be appropriate to make a winding up order under 'just and equitable' grounds by virtue of s122 Insolvency Act 1986. Success for Arthur is not guaranteed for the courts are reluctant to order the drastic remedy of winding up a solvent and viable company.

A less drastic and perhaps more attractive 'alternative' would be for Arthur to seek an order under the Companies Act 1985 s459 for the majority to buy out his shareholding. In order to be eligible for this, Arthur would have to show that the affairs of the company were being conducted in a manner unfairly prejudicial to himself as he is part of the membership. Case law on this area seems to indicate that in cases of this kind the court may well be prepared to make a s459 order.

Further the Companies Act s303, allows a company to remove a director from its board by means of an ordinary resolution of the company in a general meeting; however the articles here contain a weighted voting clause in Arthur's favour. Such clauses were approved by the House of Lords in *Bushell* v *Faith* (1). Although such clauses appear to contravene the principle that a director is always removable by ordinary resolution, the House of Lords in *Bushell* v *Faith* said that the clause merely affected the way in which the votes were counted on such a resolution, and therefore the likelihood of its being passed did not infringe the rule that such a resolution would be effective if passed. This seems a rather subtle distinction, but nevertheless the decision is still regarded as good law.

An alternative solution which Basil and Charles have considered is to seek to remove the *Bushell* v *Faith* clause and s9 Companies Act 1985 allows a company to alter its articles by special resolution. Basil and Charles could command the necessary majority. Arthur, as shareholder will presumably challenge the alteration as not being made bona fide in the best interests for the company. As in *Greenhalgh* v *Arderne Cinemas* (3), the question to ask is whether the change benefits the aggrieved member. These authorities go to show that at least in a small company, the majority have to show due regard to the interests of the minority. Although on the face of it this seems a convincing solution, the difficulty here is that the company was set up on the basis that the directors would be protected from removal and the position is a finely balanced one. Basil and Charles are by no means certain to succeed in their actions.

The last possibility is an issue of further shares so as to reduce Arthur's holding to a level where the *Bushell* v *Faith* clause would no longer protect him. However, ss89-96 Companies Act 1985 including pre-emption rights to existing shareholders have to be considered. Arthur will be able to exercise these rights to defeat any scheme to dilute his shareholding. Basil and Charles may try allotting non-cash consideration, or may choose to ignore the pre-emption rights. However s92 Companies Act 1985 will give Arthur the right to compensation for any loss, damage or expenses resulting from such a breach and a further challenge can be made that such an allocation was for an improper purpose: *Hogg* v *Cramphorn* (4). In such cases the court is likely to refer the matter to a general meeting to decide whether the shares have been properly allotted.

Basil and Charles, therefore, should consider buying Arthur's shares and can refer the purchase price to arbitration in order to fix a fair price, as it seems probable that Arthur will succeed in blocking their attempts to have him removed.

References
(1) [1969] 2 Ch 438
(2) [1971] Ch 799; [1973] AC 360
(3) [1946] 1 All ER 512
(4) [1967] Ch 254

QUESTION 5

General Comment

Debentures is a fairly popular topic; however there is a twist to the question in that Henry, the main shareholder in Bat and Ball Ltd has been granted a fixed charge. Essentially the principles remain the same. Distinction has to be made between fixed and floating charges. The concept of crystallisation, registration of charges and priority of charges. Fraudulent and wrongful trading are also relevant though fraud maybe difficult to prove.

Skeleton Solution

Liquidation retrospective to date of petition – distinguish between fixed and floating charges and registration of charges – concept of crystallisation – fixed charge takes priority unless caught by automatic crystallisation clause, only happens if later chargee has actual notice of earlier clauses – IA 1986 s245 may invalidate floating charge, not applicable to fixed charges – fraudulent and wrongful trading relevant – order of payment.

Suggested Solution

In a liquidation money must be paid out in a strict order of priority. The first payment is the costs and expenses of liquidation, then the fixed chargees, followed by preferential creditors and lastly floating chargees and any payments due to unsecured creditors. The liquidation is deemed to have commenced on the date of the petition ie November 1990. The liquidator will be concerned to establish the priority of payment to be made in the liquidation.

It is clear that Henry has a fixed charge since this charge was created in the middle of 1989. This fixed charge created by the company is registrable under Companies Act 1985 s395, and it is assumed that it was duly registered within 21 days. However, in so far as the charge relates to land it also requires to be registered under the Land Charges Act 1972. Failure to comply with this requirement will render the charge void against a subsequent purchaser for value of the legal estate. If this criterion is not met both the company and any officer in default is liable to a fine. This is because most companies obtain much of their finance from debentures secured by charges and it is important that people dealing with the company are able to find out which assets are subject to charges.

There is a possibility that Henry's fixed charge has priority over Midwest Bank's floating charge which would only have become a fixed charge on the petition of the winding up order. However, in causing the company to grant him a fixed charge, Henry is clearly infringing Insolvency Act 1986 s239, by giving a preference to one creditor of the company (ie himself) ahead of other creditors. Such a preference will accordingly be void, and Henry may be required to repay the money to the company.

The liquidator should also be advised to bear in mind ss213 and 214 IA 1986 where a director of a company incurs personal liability for 'fraudulent trading' ie trading in such a way as fraudulently to prefer one creditor over another. The provisions also deal with 'wrongful trading' ie continuing to trade knowing that the company is insolvent. There is sufficient evidence to indicate that Henry will find himself liable under both these provisions. Under the statutory predecessors of these provisions, a narrow view was taken of the concepts of 'defrauding' and 'fraudulent purpose': *Re Patrick and Lyon* (1), but it should not be assumed that the same approach would be taken at the present day, as the courts' attitude seems to have hardened somewhat with regard to such indiscretions. A misfeasance summons may be taken through the company by the liquidator under s212 IA 1986 against the accountant as he has a contractual relationship with the company and owes it a duty of care and was negligent in advising Henry to continue trading, when there was clear evidence that Bat and Ball Ltd was tottering on insolvency. However, success as to the outcome of such an action is debatable.

The floating charge granted in favour of Midwest Bank needs considering. The general concept of a floating charge was explained in *Re Yorkshire Woolcombers* (2) as a charge over assets present and future. Because these assets would in the ordinary course of business change, the charge to remain floating until some event occurs which causes crystallisation. The events which are normally regarded as causing crystallisation are the appointment of a receiver and the commencement of a wind up: *Re Victoria Steamboats* (3). The difficulty is to decide on the validity of express clauses which make crystallisation happen on the occurrence of certain specified events, ie automatic crystallisation clauses. The point does not seem to be settled in English law, but the decision of Hoffmann J in *Re Brightlife* (4) gives some support for the recognition of these clauses in English law.

In any event there is a possibility that Midwest Bank's charge is invalidated by IA 1986 s245. This provides that where in the twelve months before the commencement of a winding up, a floating charge is created and the company was insolvent immediately after the creation, the charge will be invalid except to the extent that fresh consideration was given for it. In other words such a charge cannot be used to secure pre-existing borrowing. It is arguable that no fresh consideration was provided by Midwest Bank as the floating charge was merely the re-financing of the company's debts to the bank, and if this argument is accepted, then s245 will apply, and the charge will be invalidated.

Thus the payout in the liquidation are (in order): costs and expenses of the liquidation, the preferential creditors (including Henry's wages in the previous four months preceding the liquidation, the Inland Revenue, DSS and others). Then the floating charge to Midwest Bank, followed by Henry's charge to the extent that they have not been invalidated.

References

(1) [1933] Ch 786
(2) [1904] AC 355
(3) [1897] 1 Ch 158
(4) [1987] Ch 200

QUESTION 6

General Comment

The question involves consideration of several areas and covers directors' fiduciary duties. This includes directors avoiding situations of conflict of interest and duty to the company. *Percival* v *Wright* (1) needs mentioning and contravention of s317 CA 1985 and accountability of profits made by Donald, Edward and Fred.

Skeleton Solution

Directors duties owed to company only – consider implications of *Percival* v *Wright* – accountability for personal profit by Donald, Edward and Fred – breach of s317 – breach of fiduciary duty to act for the benefit of the company.

Suggested Solution

The fiduciary duties owed by directors are basically similar to those applying to any other fiduciary relationship eg, between agent and principal or trustee and beneficiary. They are based upon the principle that since the company places its trust with the directors, they must display the utmost good faith towards the company they are dealing with or on its behalf.

Such fiduciary duties are owed to the company alone, in particular he owes no such duty to the shareholder: this was set out in *Percival* v *Wright* (1). This general principle has been somewhat modified by subsequent authority. Where the shares are held by only a few people as in *Coleman* v *Myers* (2), or where there is a special situation as in a takeover *Briess* v *Woolley* (3), directors may be held to owe a limited duty of care to the shareholder. There is a possibility this approach will be taken in modern law today.

However, the content of this duty must not be such as to create a conflict with the directors fiduciary duties to the company. Section 309 CA 1985 states that the directors when performing their functions must have regard to the interests of the members as well as the employees. The members may therefore wish to object to an act which may not be beneficial to them. Nevertheless, the directors may be able to refute this objection, as they may consider it as good industrial practice and more advantageous to the company in the long run.

Hence, the resolution passed by the directors of Elite Properties plc preventing the passing of a resolution by the shareholders to discuss the company's failure to purchase the site is within their discretion, as they were concerned that the acquisition of this site might pose long term problems for the company. The directors of Elite do not have to maximise economic benefit to the company, as they felt they were acting for the benefit of the company as a whole. Moreover, the rule in *Foss* v *Harbottle* (4) would prevent the shareholders from bringing an action, as the wrong is done to the company and it is for the company to decide what action to take. The company would be the proper plaintiff in such an action.

A director who is anyway interested in a contract with the company must declare the nature of his interest at a board meeting: s317 CA 1985. Donald, Edward and Fred would have clearly contravened this requirement and are personally liable to a fine as they made no mention of their interests in the acquisition of the site rejected by Elite Properties plc.

Further, directors have a fiduciary duty not to use either corporate information or opportunity to make an undisclosed personal profit. In *Industrial Development Consultants* v *Cooley* (5), the managing director of IDC feigned illness to secure the termination of his contract. He then took out a contract in his own name which he had unsuccessfully tried to obtain for the company. Courts held he had to account to IDC with his profits. This was also illustrated in the case of *Boston Deep Sea Fishing Co* v *Ansell* (6).

There is however a Commonwealth authority supporting the proposition that a director may retain a profit derived from an opportunity that the company has considered and rejected. In the Canadian case of *Peso Silver Mines* v *Cropper* (7), Peso's board considered and rejected the chance to purchase prospecting claims near the company's land. One of Peso's directors bought shares in a new company which was subsequently formed to purchase these claims. The courts held he did not have to account for his profits. This decision has been widely criticised by academics and has been described by Professor Gower as 'unsatisfactory and undesirable'.

The outcome of the call made on Donald, Edward and Fred to account for all the profit made as shareholders and directors of Speculative Enterprises Ltd would be influenced by several factors in light of *Peso's* case. This would include the percentage of shares held by Donald, Edward and Fred in Speculative Enterprises Ltd respectively. Other factors would be the part played by all three in the board's decision to reject the site and whether there is any link between the two transactions.

It is submitted, however, that Elite Properties plc will have a good cause of action to make Donald, Edward and Fred personally accountable for the percentage of profits made as shareholders cum directors of Speculative Enterprises Ltd. They have clearly taken advantage of a commercial opportunity as a result of being directors of Elite Properties plc.

References
(1) [1902] 2 Ch 421
(2) [1977] 2 NZLR 225, 298
(3) [1954] AC 333
(4) (1843) 2 Hare 461
(5) [1972] 1 WLR 443
(6) (1888) 39 Ch D 339
(7) (1966) 58 DLR (2d) 1

QUESTION 7

General Comment

The ultra vires doctrine and implications of s35 CA 1985 are relevant to this question. Clearly the borrowing of the money from the bank was applied for purposes not within the ambit of the objects clause of Mainstream Ltd. Lorna and Mary have delegated management to Keith: *International Sales & Agencies Ltd* v *Marcus* (1) is relevant here. Keith is personally liable for breach of his fiduciary relationship with the company.

Skeleton Solution

Taking of loan outside ambit of the objects clause – generally an ultra vires contract is void – s108 CA 1989 abolishes this as far as outsiders are concerned – delegation of management – personal liability of Keith – options available for Lorna and Mary as shareholders cum directors of Mainstream Ltd.

Suggested Solution

The ultra vires doctrine states that a company incorporated under a statute derives its objects and powers from its memorandum of association and can only pursue the objectives stated therein. The taking of the loan of £50,000 by Mainstream Ltd clearly does not fall within the objects clause and further the articles of association restrict any borrowing by the company except where sanctioned by a resolution of the directors. As Keith is the only director who has sanctioned the loan, it may be concluded that the loan is ultra vires.

However, s35 CA 1985 provides in favour of a person dealing with the company in good faith, and any such transactions are deemed to be free of any limitations contained in the memorandum of association. Moreover, s35(2) CA 1985 contains further provisions that good faith is presumed, unless the contrary is proved. The Companies Act 1989 has made very significant changes to the ultra vires rules and s108 CA 1989 abolishes this doctrine of ultra vires as far as outsiders are concerned.

The bank is clearly dealing with Mainstream Ltd and there is no suggestion of bad faith here. The difficulty is to decide whether this transaction was decided upon by all the directors. In this case,

Lorna and Mary have an understanding with Keith to carry out the day to day management of the company and as managing director, he exercises all the powers of the board. A decision by him may be treated as a decision of the directors as a whole: *International Sales Ltd v Marcus* (1). Moreover, here it is thought that *Turquand's Case* (2) will probably assist the bank, since it need not be concerned with the internal arrangements of the company, and is entitled to assume that all internal acts have been duly carried out. In view of this, it would be difficult for Mainstream Ltd to contend that the loan is ultra vires and therefore void. The rule in *Turquand's Case* only protects outsiders, therefore Lorna and Mary cannot rely upon it: *Howard v Patent Ivory Manufacturing Co* (3). They are technically caught in a dilemma, as they have effectively delegated management to Keith.

In the absence of suspicious circumstances, directors are entitled to trust the company's officers (ie Keith), to perform their duties properly; Lorna and Mary may not be liable for the acts of Keith unless they have participated in the wrongdoing. From the facts, this does not seem to be the case; further, under s727 CA 1985, the court has power in an action against an officer for breach of duty to grant relief where he has acted honestly and reasonably. Success may be dependent on whether the directors have taken legal advice: *Re Claridges' Patent Asphalte Co* (4). If this argument is accepted, Lorna and Mary may be able to avail themselves to this defence.

Keith will not be able to do so, for as a director of the company he has a fiduciary duty to act for the benefit of the company. He applied the loan to purchase shares in Highlight Ltd, which concentrates on publishing pornographic literature, a company of which he is director. This goes completely against the spirit of the objects clause of Mainstream Ltd whose main purpose is to manufacture and distribute reading material to children under seven.

As s108 CA 1989 could be used as a vehicle for fraud (directors exceeding the limits placed upon their powers could bind the company into a transaction from which they (the directors) would derive a personal benefit), s109 CA 1989 was enacted to relieve the company should this happen. The provision provides that such transactions are voidable at the option of the company and any director who authorised such a transaction is liable to indemnify the company for any loss or damage. Mainstream Ltd would be successful in an action against Keith for acting mala fide and applying the loan to invest in a company whose shares now prove worthless. Keith would be liable to indemnify Mainstream Ltd for any loss sustained by the company. He may have a defence if he can show he took all reasonable steps to secure the company's compliance or was not aware of any contravention. It is submitted that this is a very heavy burden for Keith to discharge and he would fail on both counts.

Lorna and Mary may wish to consider a derivative action for fraud on the minority, as Keith misappropriated company funds, but they would be more successful if they petitioned for an order under s459 CA 1985 complaining that the affairs of the company were conducted in a way unfairly prejudicial to them. But such drastic action may be unwarranted if they wish to keep Mainstream Ltd as a going business concern.

References
(1)   [1982] 3 All ER 551
(2)   (1856) 6 E & B 327; [1843–60] All ER Rep 435
(3)   (1888) 38 Ch D 156
(4)   [1921] 1 Ch 543

QUESTION 8

General Comment

The question deals with preferential shares and such class rights. The general rule is that all shares rank equally unless divided into class shares. Rules on reduction of capital need consideration and the interest of creditors, shareholders and the public at large must be considered. The difficulty is that class rights of preference shareholders may not be adequately protected. Issue of payment of dividends is not a compulsory requirement on companies.

Skeleton Solution

Where reduction of capital is concerned the interests of creditor, shareholders and public at large must be considered – Difficulty is that class rights of preference shareholders may not be adequately protected – Reduction of capital needs authorisation by the courts – Articles allow a challenge of such a variation. Rules on dividends – only available out of profit – discretion can be exercised – repayment not mandatory.

Suggested Solution

Alan and Benjamin are proposing to reduce the capital of the company in order to repay preference shareholders in full and thus eliminating such shares. A preference share normally carries certain preferential rights in respect of these matters, but does not normally carry a right to vote at a general meeting. Prima facie all shares rank equally: *Birch* v *Cropper* (1), but once they have been divided into classes each class of shares has different rights attached to it: *Scottish Insurance Corporation* v *Wilsons and Clyde Coal Co Ltd* (2).

The real objection to Alan and Ben's planned reduction of capital will come from Carol who is a preference shareholder. The general principle in such cases is that the shareholder must be treated according to the rights they would enjoy on winding up: *Scottish Insurance* v *Wilsons and Clyde Coal Co* (2). Moreover, the courts will also ensure that the reduction is equitable between the various classes of shareholders involved: *Re Holders Investment Trust* (3).

Generally, the court is predisposed to grant confirmation of reduction of capital under s135 CA 1985 which requires the passing of a special resolution, and such confirmation will be granted so long as the interests of the creditors are adequately protected: *Poole v National Bank of China* (4). The interests of the shareholder will be considered next, followed by the interests of the public at large. In practice, it is rare for confirmation to be refused, and Lord Cooper has gone so far to describe the confirmation procedure merely as a 'rubber stamp'.

However, if the shareholders' rights are not respected there is a risk that confirmation will be refused and in two cases shareholders' objections have led to the refusal of confirmation: *Re Old Silkstone Collieries* (5) and *Re Holders Investment Trust* (3). In both cases the reason was that class rights had not been respected. It appears therefore that confirmation may be given only if the courts can be persuaded that the scheme proposed by Alan and Benjamin is fair and this is a very heavy burden to discharge, as Carol is wholly opposed to their proposal and she will be within her rights as preferential shareholder to veto such a proposal.

Alternatively Alan and Benjamin may consider issuing further shares with identical rights to existing preference shares and calling a class meeting of preferential shareholders which could then vote in favour of their proposal for repayment. However, such an allotment of shares must be made for a proper purpose otherwise it is liable to be set aside by the courts: *Hogg v Cramphorn* (6). The major problem facing Alan and Benjamin will be the validity of a resolution passed at a class meeting of preferential shareholders. The test laid down in *Allen v Gold Reefs of West Africa* (7) is whether the resolution is passed bona fide for the benefit of the class as a whole. The consent of the preferential shareholders is required under CA 1985 s125(2), since the scheme proposed involves a variation of their rights. Some of the preferential shareholders are also ordinary shareholders in this case. It is submitted that the resolution of the class meeting if passed will be open to challenge because it appears that those voting in favour of the resolution did so in order to benefit themselves as ordinary shareholders rather than to benefit the preferential shareholders as a whole. Alan and Benjamin would stand little success in achieving their aims.

Although Rain and Sun Ltd have been making profits, no dividends have been declared. The general rule is that dividends are payments made out of profits to the shareholders. Dividends paid to preferential shareholders will be at a fixed rate whereas dividends paid to ordinary shareholders will vary according to the prosperity of the company. Shareholders do not have an automatic right to dividends even if profits are available as the directors may consider it more prudent to retain profits within the company. Therefore a dividend is not a debt of the company until it is declared, and even then on liquidation it is not payable until after all the outside creditors have been paid. It would be difficult therefore for Carol to insist that dividends be paid.

Finally, it may be worth advising Alan and Benjamin of the possibility of using the provisions for re-purchasing of shares under ss162-164 CA 1985. However, the articles will have to be altered to give a power to purchase the shares and a special resolution would have to be passed to authorise such a purchase.

References

(1)   (1889) 14 App Cas 525
(2)   [1949] AC 462
(3)   [1971] 2 All ER 289
(4)   [1907] AC 229
(5)   [1954] Ch 169
(6)   [1967] Ch 254
(7)   [1900] 1 Ch 656

UNIVERSITY OF LONDON
LLB EXAMINATION 1992
PART II for External Students

COMPANY LAW

Wednesday, 3 June: 2.30 pm to 5.30 pm

Answer *FOUR* of the following EIGHT questions, including at least ONE from Section A and at least TWO from Section B.

SECTION A

1   'A major achievement of company law reform over the past decade has been the replacement of the old section 210 [of the Companies Act 1948] with, first section 75 [of the Companies Act 1980], and now section 459 [of the Companies Act 1985]. This has transformed a provision from which the judges systematically removed all the teeth into one which now bites deep into the administration of small private companies. We can now truly say that we have proper protection for minority shareholders – an indispensable ingredient to fairness in the principles of company law.'
    Discuss.

2   'There are many examples of conduct in the administration of companies which are controlled both by being criminalised by statute as well as being remediable by civil suit at the instance of the victim. Yet in the case of insider trading, there is only a criminal penalty. If insider trading is to be effectively brought to an end, it is essential that a civil remedy should be provided.'
    Discuss.

3   'It may have taken over a hundred years, but the Financial Services Act 1986 has finally solved the problem of providing an adequate remedy for someone who suffers damage through an investment in a public company and who was induced to make that investment by a material misrepresentation.'
    Discuss.

SECTION B

4   Basil and Brenda have for many years been active in the business of property development. They are the directors of Alpha Limited and own about 65% of the shares. The remainder of the shares are spread among some 7 or 8 shareholders who take little or no part in the running of the company. Basil and Brenda were also directors of Delta Limited, a company in which they held all the shares but which was recently placed in creditors' voluntary winding up and in which there is a substantial deficit such that creditors can expect no more than 15 pence in the pound.

The main business of both companies was (and is) the purchase of suitable property, its redevelopment for either commercial or residential use and then its sale. Despite the downturn in the economy, Basil and Brenda continued throughout 1990 and 1991 with an aggressive purchasing policy. They were advised on several occasions by the companies' auditors to slow down, but they rejected this advice. This policy led directly to the insolvent liquidation of Delta Limited and, although it seems that this will be avoided in the case of Alpha Limited, that company has suffered huge losses. There will be no dividends for years to come.

These problems were increased by the huge donations of £50,000 which Basil and Brenda caused Alpha Limited to make to the Conservative Party in 1989 and again in 1990. Basil and Brenda have considerable private means and the following transaction has also recently come to light. In the middle of 1991, before the liquidation of Delta Limited, Basil and Brenda learned of the sale of a property in North London for £150,000. As it would have been difficult to raise the finance through either Alpha or Delta, Basil and Brenda bought this property in their own names. It now turns out that this property is much more valuable than anticipated since the Local Authority has unexpectedly allowed redevelopment of this property without any restrictions. As a result Basil and Brenda are planning to sell this property for £350,000.

Advise the liquidator of Delta Limited and the minority shareholders of Alpha Limited. (Ignore the statutory remedies under section 459 of the Companies Act 1985 and section 122(1)(g) of the Insolvency Act 1986.)

5   Sam Sandcastle was the sole director and shareholder (apart from one share held by his wife) of Grand Illusions Limited ('the

company'), a company which specialised in the manufacture and sale of jewellery. Some of this jewellery was manufactured by Sam himself under an agreement between himself and the company, some was manufactured by jewellers who sold their items to the company and some was imported by the company from abroad. The company had also entered into agreements with Denis Diamond and Pearl Pond to take their entire output of manufactured jewellery.

The company has been badly hit by the recession and the overdraft with the Bank of Cash and Credit ('the bank') climbed to £300,000 by the end of 1991. The bank demanded security and in February Sam caused the company to grant a floating charge over all its undertaking to the bank as well as a fixed charge over all its book debts. Despite hectic trading in the period from February to May, the company's fortunes continued to decline.

In May, the Bank undertook an investigation of the company's affairs and discovered:

a) that the company had a substantial amount of manufactured jewellery which when the economy improves will probably be saleable at substantial profits;

b) that the company had taken delivery of large quantities of the raw material necessary for the manufacture of jewellery, but that much of this had been supplied under contracts with retention of title provisions;

c) that Sam had caused the company to pay him £50,000 in part reduction of a loan made by Sam to the company in 1990 and in part payment for jewellery made by Sam and sold to the company;

d) that the company owed Pearl and Denis each about £10,000;

e) that the Inland Revenue was pressing for payment of Corporation Tax arrears of some £50,000;

f) that in 1991 the company entered into an agreement with the Easy Financing Company, in terms of which all sales abroad by the company were to go through the Finance Company in exchange for 90% of the invoiced price and that all payments made to the company in respect of such sales were to be received by the company as agent for the Finance Company.

A petition has now been presented for the appointment of an administrator to the Company. The company's total assets are probably not worth more than £100,000 but there are signs of considerable improvement in the economy.

Advise the bank whether:

i) to accede to this petition, or

ii) to appoint an administrative receiver, or

iii) to oppose the petition in favour of a winding up petition.

6 Henry and Isobel decided to go into business together. They decided to conduct their business through the medium of a limited liability company and instructed Jane, a solicitor, to register a company called Joint Engineering Ventures ('the company'). Jane advised them that the process would take about six weeks. Henry and Isobel also mentioned to Jane that they would need certain computer equipment and machinery and discussed with Jane the best way of finding this equipment, as well as how best to raise the capital that would be necessary for the company. Henry and Isobel, who were becoming increasingly dependent on Jane for commercial advice, asked Jane to become a director of the company but she declined.

Henry then arranged for the lease of suitable premises, taking the lease in his name with the understanding that the company would become the lessee as soon as it was registered. He paid a deposit of £5,000. He and Isobel were persuaded by Kevin, a computer salesman, to purchase equipment for £15,000. They also entered into a contract for the purchase of engineering machinery from Engineering Equipment Ltd for £7,500, signing the contract 'Henry and Jane as purchasers for and on behalf of Joint Engineering Venture Ltd (in formation)'.

When the company was registered, Henry and Isobel took Jane's advice to take a long term loan with the Easy Loans Finance Company (in preference to a regular overdraft). The articles of association – which had been drafted by Jane – included a clause (regulation 51) requiring the company to take over all obligations undertaken by 'Henry, Isobel and Jane in connection with the formation of the company'. At the first directors' meeting, a resolution confirming the articles of association and in particular regulation 51 was passed.

The company did not prosper. Three months after registration, it went into insolvent liquidation. The liquidator has established that:

a) apart from the resolution referred to, no steps were taken to transfer the lease to the company;

b) Henry has lodged a claim with the liquidator for money laid out as a deposit under the lease;

c) Jane has lodged a claim for 'solicitors' fees in connection with the formation of (the company)' for £7,500;

d) Jane had, without telling Henry and Isobel, arranged for Kevin to approach Henry and Isobel and had received a commission of £1,500 (as agreed with Kevin – 10% of any sales made);

e) the loan facilities with the Easy Loans Finance Company cost the company £1,500 more than a regular overdraft would have done;

f) the engineering equipment has risen dramatically in value owing to a worldwide shortage. It is now worth £20,000. Henry and Isobel are claiming to be personally entitled to it. Engineering Equipment is claiming return of the machines supplied.

Discuss.

7 Health Industries plc is a large well-established drug company which is the head of a large group of companies including Property Limited, a wholly-owned subsidiary which owns all the premises used by Health Industries in its business, and Testing Limited, another wholly owned subsidiary which was set up specifically to carry out commercially risky ventures in the search for profitable new drugs. The Board of Directors of Health Industries consists of seven members, but the managing director, Larry Lincoln, is the dominant force. The board generally agrees with his proposals and he has become clearly associated in the mind of the public with Health Industries plc.

Last year the local authority governing the area where Health Industries carries on part of its business expropriated certain land under its statutory powers as part of a slum clearance programme. This included land owned by Property Limited. The compensation offered under the scheme established by the expropriating statute provided for compensation to be paid to 'the owner of the expropriated land according to the open market value of the land plus the assessed damages for any loss of profits suffered by the owner'. The compensation offered by the local authority to Property Limited has ignored the loss, amounting the £150,000, suffered by Health Industries plc in having to relocate its operations elsewhere.

More recently, Testing Limited undertook experiments to try to develop a drug to cure certain types of cancer. In a high profile advertising campaign, Larry Lincoln made a personal appeal on behalf of Testing Limited for volunteers for this experiment. The advertising campaign ran for several days on television and in national newspapers, and 100 volunteers were selected. The experiment went disastrously wrong; several volunteers died, others were permanently maimed. The experiment was not properly researched and there is clear evidence of negligence. Testing Limited has assets of £2,000 to £3,000 and now faces claims of several millions. Test cases have been brought against both Testing Limited and Health Industries plc.

Advise Health Industries plc.

8 The share capital of Valhalla Limited ('the company') consists of 60,000 £1 shares which are held as to 15,000 by Alan, 12,500 each by Barry, Colin and Donald (all four of whom are directors) and 7,500 spread among five different investors who take no interest in the affairs of the company but who may be relied upon to vote as instructed by Barry. Originally the company was carried on by Barry, Colin and Donald, but when they arranged for the company to buy Alan's business, this was paid for by the issue to Alan of 15,000 shares. On this occasion as part of the agreement under which Alan's business was purchased, the articles of association of the company were altered so as to include the following clause:

> 'No resolution by the board of directors of the company, or by the company itself, which concerns the acquisition or disposition of property for a price in excess of £100,000, shall be valid unless agreed to by any shareholder holding more than 20% of the issued share capital of the company.'

Barry, Colin and Donald are now anxious to expand the property development operations of the company and recently proposed the purchase of a corner site for £1m for redevelopment. Alan voted against this proposal. Barry, Colin and Donald are concerned that Alan will veto the proposed expansion of the company's business and have been searching for ways in which Alan's entrenched veto might be eliminated.

Advise them.

PART A
QUESTION 1

General Comment

The topic of minority shareholder protection in company law is always a popular question. It can be easily dressed up as a problem question, either self-contained or as part of a larger problem question, and also lends itself to analysis in an essay. This essay question is relatively easy to pass since it is only really asking for consideration of s459 in any detail and is thus confined in scope. In order to do well though the topic should have been fully considered and read around.

Skeleton Solution

Old provision of s210 Companies Act CA 1948.

Need for reform.

s75 CA 1980 and s459 CA 1985.

Major differences.

Description of s459 in operation with case law illustrations.

Assessment of its efficacy.

Suggested Solution

Prior to the enactment of s210 Companies Act 1948 (on the recommendation of the Cohen Committee) the only remedy available to a minority shareholder who felt his interests were being threatened by the actions of the majority shareholders in the way they were running the company was the somewhat drastic remedy of petitioning for a winding up on the grounds that it was 'just and equitable'. This solution is still, of course, available and found in s122 (1)(g) Insolvency Act 1986 but is far from satisfactory since it means an otherwise viable business is dissolved perhaps in conditions in which it will not be possible to realise the best price for the company's assets and the minority shareholder may not fully realise the true extent of his interest, apart from it being a very 'all or nothing' type of solution. Section 210 was designed to empower the court to provide discretionary relief to a minority shareholder in a situation where the affairs of a company were being conducted in such a manner as to be oppressive to a minority shareholder. The facts had to be such, however, that they could also justify a winding up petition being granted, had one been sought, on the just and equitable ground. In spite of an auspicious start with the two successful petitions under s210 in *Scottish Co-operative Wholesale Society* v *Meyer* (1) and *Re H R Harmer Ltd* (2) the section quickly lost its effect through narrow judicial interpretation of 'oppression' and various procedural hurdles placed in its way. In order to constitute oppressive conduct the actions of the majority had to be extremely harsh, at the very least improper. There also had to be a continuing pattern of oppressive conduct so that one or two isolated incidents, no matter how unfair and harsh an effect they might have on the minority shareholder, would not be enough for a s210 petition to succeed.

Further reform was necessary and was called for by the Jenkins Committee on Company Law in 1962 but it was not until the Companies Act 1980 and s75 (now consolidated in s459 CA 1985) that s210 was overhauled. The most important change is the replacement of the requirement that the conduct of the company's affairs be oppressive with the less onerous and easier to establish requirement that 'the company's affairs are being or have been conducted in a manner which is unfairly prejudicial to the interests of some part of the members (including the [petitioner])': s459(1). Unfairly prejudicial is a more neutral and less perjorative term than oppressive, and indeed has been interpreted as such by the courts. Although the courts have been careful to leave the meaning of the term open, the most commonly quoted guidelines derive from Slade J, in *Re Bovey Hotel Ventores* (3):

> 'Without prejudice to the generality of the wording of the section, which may cover many other situations, a member of a company will be able to bring himself within the section if he can show that the value of his shareholding has been seriously diminished or at least seriously jeopardised by reason of a course of conduct on the part of those persons who have had de facto control of the company, which has been unfair to the member concerned'.

The test of unfairness is an objective one and has been used to encompass situations which are inequitable not just illegal. Other examples of unfairly prejudicial conduct include the diverting of part of a company's business away from the company and to another company owned by the majority shareholder: *Re London School of Electronics Ltd* (4).

Other improvements that s459 has wrought are; it is no longer necessary to establish such a severe business relationship breakdown that a winding up petition would also lie; there is no need to establish a course of conduct as being unfairly prejudicial since subs(1) clearly envisages a single act or omission as being capable of constituting unfair prejudice; the remedy can survive the death of a member and devolve on to his PRs (subs(2)); the Companies Act 1989 further increased the utility of s459 in that relief will now be available if it is in the interests of the members generally affected. So, just because all members suffer equally this does not prevent the section from applying.

Finally, s461 gives the court the broadest possible discretion to grant relief as the court may 'make such order as it thinks fit for giving relief in respect of the matters complained of' (s461(1)) and ⚹ goes on to give a non-exhaustive list of examples of some of the extremely useful orders it may make including an order providing for the purchase of the shares of any member by the company or by other members (one of the most commonly sought in practice) and an order authorising civil proceedings to be brought in the name of the company (an improvement on s210).

Although the workings of s459 are not without their own set of difficulties, in particular finding a fair valuation mechanism on share purchase orders (see *Virdi* v *Abbey Leisure Ltd* (5)), it has proved a vast improvement on its predecessor and is a popular and effective alternative to a s122(1)(g) Insolvency Act 1986 application or struggling with the difficulties of coming within the 'fraud on a minority' exception to the rule in *Foss* v *Harbottle* (6).

References
(1) [1959] AC 324
(2) [1959] 1 WLR 62
(3) (Ch D 21 July 1981) Unreported but see *Re R A Noble & Sons (Clothing) Ltd* [1983] BCLC 273
(4) [1986] 2 Ch 211
(5) [1990] BCLC 342
(6) (1843) 2 Hare 461

⚹ Sec 461(2)(i) – form of relief that may be used – overcomes problems with FvH.

QUESTION 2

General Comment

This question is not, as it may seem to some, simply asking for a straightforward exposition of the law on insider dealing. Such an answer, while it might pass if comprehensive and accurate, would not earn a good mark. Instead it is asking you to think more deeply and critically about the market phenomenon of insider dealing and how the law should best (if at all) control it and prevent it.

Skeleton Solution

Examples of conduct statutorily criminalised and also remediable civilly.

Outline of criminal penalty for insider trading.

Assessment of efficacy.

Arguments for and against proscription of insider trading.

Utility of a civil remedy for 'victim'.

Reforms in consequence of EC Directive.

Suggested Solution

Company law is awash with instances of multiple layers of legal protection in that the Companies Act 1985 renders criminal many specific acts and omissions of directors (imposing fines and in some cases the possibility of imprisonment) which will also be of relevance in a civil action by the company itself against the directors. An example is the prohibited loans to directors' provisions in s330 Companies Act 1985, contravention of which by a director can result in criminal liability under s342 and civil liability under s341 in that a director must account for any gain to the company and indemnify the company against any loss or damage. A general action for breach of fiduciary duty will also be available for a company against its directors in many cases where they have committed other specific statutory offences – for example s206 Insolvency Act 1986 (fraud in anticipation of winding up).

The criminal prohibition on insider dealing, however, although it is wide in the category of persons to whom it can apply (including not just directors but also a number of others concerned in the administration of companies including recipients of inside information or 'tippees'), is not specifically backed up with any civil remedy to compensate the victim of an insider trader. The prohibition is contained in the Company Securities (Insider Dealing) Act 1985 and applies to dealing in securities on a recognised stock exchange on the basis of unpublished price-sensitive information. The offence also extends to counselling or procuring someone else to deal on the basis of such information and communicating such information to another person in circumstances where one has reasonable cause to believe that that other person will use it for dealing or in turn further counselling and procuring. Thus rings and networks of insiders are technically within the legislation. It is not just persons connected with the company (most obviously directors, officers and advisers privy to sensitive information) who are within the scope of the offence. It extends to individuals who 'knowingly obtain (directly or indirectly)' such information from a person connected with the company (secondary insiders or tippees); individuals contemplating a takeover offer for a particular company (always a lucrative opportunity for an insider) and their tippees; and persons who obtain and abuse inside information obtained in an official capacity eg the DTI official who abuses confidential government information about a particular company. The consequences of contravention of the Act are purely criminal though s8 imposes up to seven years imprisonment and/or a fine. In fact s8(3) expressly provides there are to be no effects on the validity of transactions in contravention of the Act and nowhere does the Act provide for any specific civil remedy for the victim(s) of an insider trader.

The enforcement and efficacy of the Act have been criticised and the 1989 Companies Act contained amendments designed to improve regulatory performance. It is sometimes argued that the courts have been hesitant to use their power of imprisonment and fines have been too light, and that a civil remedy which somehow required the insider to disgorge his profits (as pertains in the USA) would have an additional deterrent effect. However the whole idea of a specific civil remedy calls for closer analysis, for who exactly is the victim of an insider trader? Is it his market counterparty? If so then couldn't it be argued that they suffered no actual loss since they were willing to make the trade when they bought from or sold to the insider at that price? Is the victim the company whose securities are the subject of insider trading? If so then what is the actual damage suffered by that company for listed securities are bought and sold daily for a thousand different reasons? Some commentators have even argued that insider trading is efficient since it improves the rate of dissemination of new information to the market and hence benefits efficiency. At the moment the only sustainable legal argument that a civil remedy exists can be made in the limited circumstances where the insider owes a fiduciary duty to Company A (eg he is a director of Company A) and in the course of the discharge and performance of his duty he comes into possession of unpublished price sensitive information about the securities of Company B. If he deals on his own behalf on the basis of that information then it can be argued that he is liable to account for any gain he makes to Company A in action for breach of fiduciary duty brought by Company A against him: *Regal (Hastings) Ltd* v *Gulliver* (1) and *Phipps* v *Boardman* (2). In addition a counterparty to an insider trade could always try and argue fraudulent misrepresentation.

The introduction of a specific statutory remedy which would work to the benefit of a broader range of 'victims' is not imminent since recent law reform proposals to be contained soon in legislation implementing the EEC Directive coordinating regulations on insider dealing (3) expressly rejected the idea of a civil remedy on the grounds that the potential for civil action mentioned above is adequate (4).

References
(1) [1942] 1 All ER 378
(2) [1964] 2 All ER 187
(3) Council Directive of 13 XI 1989
(4) Para 2.12 DTI Consultative Document *The Law on Insider Trading* 1989.

QUESTION 3

General Comment

This is quite a difficult question in that it requires critical analysis of the solution offered by the Financial Services Act 1986 to the problem of compensating those misled into investing in a public company. This basic objective of investor protection is one with which company law has long been preoccupied and as capital markets become more complicated it becomes in turn more complex to fulfil. You should not attempt to answer this question unless you have a clear understanding of the new statutory regimes and remedies the FSA introduced for listed and unlisted securities offerings as well as the common law remedies which continue to exist.

Skeleton Solution

Gaps in 'old law'.

Section 67 Companies Act 1985.

Definition of 'prospectus'.

New statutory regimes for public offers of listed securities (Part IV FSA) and unlisted securities (Part V FSA).

New statutory remedies ss150 and 166 FSA.

Persons liable to pay compensation.

Defences available to responsible persons.

Measure of damages.

Continuing common law remedies preserved.

Suggested Solution

Prior to the Financial Services Act (FSA) 1986 the Companies Act requirements relating to public issues and prospectuses did not apply at all to the listed securities markets ie those securities admitted to the Stock Exchange's official list – the tightest and most difficult to enter UK public capital market. The Companies Act 1985 (Part 3 ss56–79, the prospectus provisions) only applied to the Unlisted Securities Market and the 'over the counter' market for securities. This meant that there were disparities in the different regimes for public issues and defects arose such as the fact that the prospectus provisions of the Companies Act were interpreted to apply only to offers for the subscription or purchase of securities for cash. Since most takeover offers are structured for non-cash consideration then they fell outside the investor protection regime.

The Financial Services Act 1986 aims to rationalise and put on a more level footing the disclosure and compensation provisions relating to the Stock Exchange's official listed market and the other markets in which the public is induced to part with its money by way of investing in company shares. Historically investor protection in the former had been good whereas it left much to be desired in the latter.

Part IV FSA deals with the admission of securities of a public company to the official list of the Stock Exchange. It designates the Stock Exchange as the competent authority for the purposes of making listing rules, and applying them to determine whether a company fulfils the criteria contained therein. The Act talks of prescribed listing particulars rather than using the term 'prospectus', the Stock Exchange should ensure that its listing rules require in particular that listing particulars contain enough information pertaining to the financial position and prospects of the company issuing securities as well as information on rights attaching to those securities to enable an investor to make a reasonably informed assessment of those matters (s146 FSA). They must be approved by the Stock Exchange and then registered with the Registrar of Companies. Part V FSA provides that an 'advertisement offering securities' must not be issued unless a prospectus document containing certain prescribed information about those particular securities has first been lodged with the companies registry. Just as with the listing particulars regime this is designed to ensure that potential investors can make the same kind of informed assessment about the company itself and the securities it is offering (s163 FSA).

What remedies exist then if despite apparent compliance with these statutory requirements the relevant listing particulars or prospectus contain information which adds up to a material misrepresentation of the true position so that an investor is misled into investing his monies where he would otherwise not have and thereby suffers loss? The principal statutory remedies are contained in s150 FSA which governs compensation for false or misleading listing particulars and s166 which governs compensation for false or misleading prospectuses and replaces s67 Companies Act 1985. Section 150 FSA imposes civil liability on the persons responsible for any listing particulars which contain false or misleading statements or omissions which in turn cause loss to any person who has acquired the securities to which the particulars relate. It is worth noting that compensation is payable under s150 to anyone who bought the securities in question even if he bought on the secondary market and did not rely directly on the listing particulars. It perhaps might be thought that s150 would award a misled investor his loss of expectation of gain as a result of the misleading statement as a measure of damages. However the Act is not clear here; in using the words 'suffers a loss' it seems that the basic tort measure of damages, viz out of pocket expenses, is being employed. This seems strange and less than satisfactory in an investment context. The persons liable to pay compensation to a misled investor are enumerated in s152 FSA as the issuer, every director or person who has given his authority to be named as a director in the listing particulars, others who have expressly assumed responsibility for the contents of the particulars, and lastly others who authorised their contents. Section 151 FSA provides defences available in a s150 compensation action which are broadly similar to those contained in the old prospectus provisions of the Companies Act (s68 1985 Act) namely, reasonable belief in the veracity of the statement, reasonable reliance on the authority of an expert, acting in an official capacity etc. It is arguable that an investor who has suffered loss and cannot proceed against any of the persons liable under s150 could proceed against the Stock Exchange itself for breach of statutory duty. The provisions for providing compensation for investors in unlisted securities are contained in ss166-168 FSA and roughly mirror those just examined. In addition here with unlisted securities if an 'authorised person' (ie authorised to do investment business under the FSA generally) contravenes s159 or s160 FSA (prospectus registration requirements) then the civil remedies enjoyed generally by the Securities and Investments Board under the FSA on behalf of investors may be invoked. Particularly valuable to the individual investor are access to the SIB compensation scheme (ss53 and 54) and the SIB's power to apply under s61 for restitution orders to benefit investors.

Finally it should be noted that ss150(4) and 166(4) expressly preserve existing common law remedies that may be of additional assistance to a misled investor aside from the statutory remedies in the FSA. These are: a common law right to rescind the contract of allotment for the securities on the basis that a material misrepresentation has been made; any rights to damages which may exist under the Misrepresentation Act 1967; and actions for deceit.

In order to be able to rescind the contract of allotment the misrepresentation must be shown to be the responsibility of the company, ie made by the directors or the company's agents: *Lynde v Anglo-Italian Hemp Co* (1) and the investor must not have lost his right to rescind by affirming the contract in any way, eg acting as a member, attending and voting at meetings etc. Rescission does not equal compensation although it will help the investor to avoid other possible liabilities (further calls to pay if shares part paid etc). Section 2(2) Misrepresentation Act 1967 may give the investor damages instead of rescission in the case of the material misrepresentation being an innocent one, and s2(1) affords a remedy in damages for negligent misrepresentation. The usual difficulties with the application of the Misrepresentation Act 1967 and ascertaining damages under it apply but there is nothing to indicate that the Act does not apply to public offers of shares. If the investor wishes to ground his action against the company in deceit he should be warned that he cannot recover damages in deceit against the company unless he also rescinds the contract of allotment of shares: *Houldsworth* v *City of Glasgow Bank* (2) Regardless of an action against the company the investor can proceed against the promoters, directors, issuers and experts responsible for the prospectus if it can be shown they acted fraudulently. The difficulties of establishing fraud at common law are legend however.

The statutory framework provided for investor compensation by Parts IV and V FSA in the event of misleading prospectus and listing particulars statements is likely to be clearer and more certain in operation than the general common law remedies and more rational and wider in application than the pre-existing Companies Act provisions although it is not likely to be without its own difficulties for judicial interpretation.

References
(1)   [1896] 1 Ch 178
(2)   (1880) 5 App Cas 317

PART B
QUESTION 4

General Comment

Although this question is concerned with the duties of directors it also embraces aspects which are only marginally within that topic. The wholly separate issue of the rule in *Foss* v *Harbottle* is also raised. The candidate's ability to summon up material gleaned from quite distinct parts of company law is also tested.

Skeleton Solution

Delta Ltd.

Possible negligence claim against directors.

Fraudulent trading.

Wrongful trading.

Alpha Ltd.

Negligence.

Ultra vires.

Fiduciary duty.

Rule in *Foss* v *Harbottle*.

Suggested Solution

As to Delta Ltd, it is possible that the directors have handled the company's affairs negligently. But the approach taken by the law in determining whether directors have been negligent could be regarded as somewhat lenient. It must first be ascertained what knowledge and experience the individual director has concerning the activity in question; having found what the knowledge and experience is, the director is then expected by law to have made a reasonable exercise of it: *Re Brazilian Rubber Plantations Ltd* (1); *Re City Equitable Fire Assurance Co* (2). It is therefore possible that one director or both directors would incur liability under this head. If a claim were to be made under this head, the liquidator would sue in the name of and on behalf of the company (s165 and Schedule 4 Part II Insolvency Act 1986).

If the company is in liquidation as is the case here and it appears that its business has been carried on with intent to defraud creditors or for any fraudulent purpose, the court may on the liquidator's application order anyone who was knowingly party to the fraudulent trading to make such contribution to the company's assets as the court thinks proper (s213 Insolvency Act 1986). The mental element in fraudulent trading requires '... real dishonesty involving, according to current notions of fair trading among commercial men at the present day, real moral blame': per Maughan J, in *Re Patrick and Lyon* (3). Claims under this head are difficult to prove and therefore infrequent.

The liquidator is much more likely to make an application under s214 alleging wrongful trading by the directors; if established, the court may order such contribution to company assets as it thinks proper. Wrongful trading is committed, if the company has gone into insolvent liquidation, by any person who at some point in time before the liquidation commenced either knew or ought to have known that there was no reasonable prospect of the company avoiding insolvent liquidation, and who was a director of the company at that time. But it is a defence to the director to show that, from the time he knew or should have known of the pending insolvency, he thereafter took every step he ought to minimise loss to the company's creditors. Moreover the facts which he ought to have known, the conclusions he should have reached and the steps he should have taken are those attributable to a reasonable diligent person having the knowledge and experience which could reasonably be expected of a person carrying on the functions of that director, plus any knowledge and experience which he in fact possessed. It should be noted that, in contrast with a common law negligence action, s214 in effect requires the director to show, as a minimum, the knowledge and experience which could reasonably be expected of a holder of that post, and irrespective of whether he in fact has such knowledge and experience.

As to the principle governing assessment of the amount of the contribution should the wrongful trading claim succeed, *Re Produce Marketing Consortium Ltd* (4) should be cited and discussed.

As to Alpha Ltd, the possibility that the directors have been negligent is as it was in respect of Beta Ltd but there will be no claim for fraudulent trading or wrongful trading, since the company is not insolvent. As to the huge donations to a political party, the company may act within the objects clause (whose precise terms we do not know) of its memorandum, and is also by implication entitled to do matters which are incidental or conducive thereto. Here the company might have express authority from its objects clause to make political gifts, but it is more probable that reliance will have to be placed on implication; in the former case the gift cannot be ultra vires (*Re Horsley and Wright Ltd* (5)), but otherwise the payment must have been for the benefit of the company, reasonably incidental to its business, and made bona fide in the interests of the company: *Re Lee, Behrens and Co* (6). Companies not infrequently make gifts to political parties whose programmes the directors regard as favourable to the commercial interests of the company.

The directors hold all their powers as fiduciaries, and must exercise them bona fide for the benefit of the company and for the purposes for which they were conferred, and must not without company authority profit from their position as directors. This will be particularly relevant to the North London land purchase; if the directors learned of the opportunity in their capacity as directors, they have profited from their position without authority to do so and should account to the company for the gains: *Regal (Hastings) Ltd v Gulliver* (7). Difficulties remain as to which company or companies the directors are accountable for the gain – it would seem both are in the relevant area of activity – and in what proportion if liable to both, and whether ratification of what has been done in general meeting would be valid, as a dictum in *Regal* suggests.

Should the directors be liable for negligence or accountable for the profit, or both, the wrong is to a corporate body or bodies, hence under the rule in *Foss v Harbottle* (8) the company is the proper plaintiff, and prima facie the only person whom the court will hear as to the merits; since in this case the directors control the company through their shareholdings the company obviously will not resolve to sue. There are exceptions to the rule; these do not extend to claims for negligence (*Pavlides v Jensen* (9)) though it may be different where the directors have personally profited from the negligence at the company's expense (*Daniels v Daniels* (10)). An exception is also made when the alleged wrongdoers control the company and are alleged to have acted fraudulently; 'fraud' here is used in a wider sense than common law fraud and includes seriously oppressive conduct: *Estmanco (Kilner House) Ltd v Greater London Council* (11).

Where the wrong is to the company but, under an exception to *Foss v Harbottle*, a shareholder is permitted to sue, he does so in what is termed a derivative action; he must also make the company a party to the suit as co-defendant, since the right of action is in truth that of the company and the court is thereby enabled to award damages or other relief, should he succeed, to the company. He must also bring a representative action, suing on behalf of himself and all other shareholders except the defendants, with the consequence that all persons involved are bound by the judgment.

References
- (1)   [1911] 1 Ch 425
- (2)   [1925] 1 Ch 407
- (3)   [1933] Ch 786
- (4)   [1989] 3 All ER 1
- (5)   [1982] 3 All ER 1045
- (6)   [1932] 2 Ch 46
- (7)   [1942] 1 All ER 378
- (8)   (1843) 2 Hare 461
- (9)   [1956] Ch 565
- (10) [1978] Ch 406
- (11) [1982] 1 WLR 2

QUESTION 5

General Comment

The question poses a good many issues concerning priority of claims to the assets of an insolvent company and the validity of its recent transactions, coupled with some comparison of administration, receivership and liquidation. Thus it could not be answered satisfactorily without having studied insolvency as a whole.

Skeleton Solution

Assets of insolvent company.

Avoidance of certain transactions.

Romalpa.

Priority of claimants.

Aspects of administration, administrative receivership and liquidation compared.

Suggested Solution

The validity of the charges to the bank should first be checked. There is unlikely to have been any failure to register under the Companies Act 1985 s398, nor is there any likelihood of a preference under s239 Insolvency Act (IA) 1986. But if the company were to commence liquidation, or a petition on which an administration order was made were to be presented, within 12 months of the creation of the floating charge, and had been unable to pay its debts at the date the charge was created, the charge would be invalidated except for money paid, or the value of goods and services supplied, at or after creation of the charge (IA s245). Although the decision in *Re Yeovil Glove Co Ltd* (1) could reduce the impact of s245 upon the floating charge to the bank, yet insofar as s245 poses a threat to the bank's position it would obviously benefit the bank to avert liquidation or the appointment of an administrator at present.

As regards the raw material supplied under the *Romalpa*-type reservation of title clauses, such clauses usually succeed insofar as the raw material is still clearly identifiable and unused; the clause may also be so worded as to succeed if the raw material has been incorporated into a larger article, provided the raw material is still readily identifiable and can be physically identified (*Hendy Lennox (Industrial Engines) Ltd* v *Graham Puttick Ltd* (2), but not if they have been blended into other goods in such a manner as to lose their identity (*Borden (UK) Ltd* v *Scottish Timber Products Ltd* (3)). The raw material, therefore, may well not be an asset of the company, but much will turn on the facts and the precise wording of the *Romalpa*-type clauses.

With regard to the payment of £50,000 made by the company to Sam, this may be a preference under s239. If a company has at a relevant time given a person a preference, the administrator or liquidator may apply to the court for an order restoring the position prior to the preference. The court is also given wide powers under s241. A creditor such as Sam is preferred if the company does anything which has the effect of putting the creditor in a better position should the company go into insolvent liquidation, but only if, also, the company was, when deciding to give the preference, influenced by a desire to better his position. Since Sam is, by virtue of his being a director of the company, a person 'connected' with it, the time of the preference will not be a 'relevant time' unless given within two years of the commencement of liquidation or the presentation of the petition on which an administration order was made, as the case may be.

The Revenue is no longer a preferential creditor, and Sam, Pearl and Denis are also ordinary creditors as to the sums listed as still owed to them. Hence the bank, insofar as it is a valid secured creditor, ranks in priority to them. A liquidator or administrative receiver must however pay any preferential creditors in priority to the holder of a floating charge.

The arrangement with Easy Financing Company appears to be neither a preference nor a security. The assignment would appear to be absolute. If so, the company could presumably only assign to Easy Financing such interest in the book debts as the company then had.

As indicated, the appointment of a liquidator or administrator may invalidate the floating charge to the bank wholly or in part; conversely a liquidator or administrator could seek court orders setting aside preferences. Appointment of an administrative receiver would not endanger the security conferred by the floating charge, but an administrative receiver is not empowered to have preferences set aside. The bank must choose its course according to the relative sums, dates and risks involved.

References

(1) [1965] Ch 148
(2) [1984] 1 All ER 152
(3) [1981] Ch 25

QUESTION 6

General Comment

The topics of the effect of pre-incorporation contracts and the duties owed by company promoters are fairly popular and almost always crop up together. Although not too difficult if these topics have been fully revised it is a long question so a well organised and structured answer is necessary. The way in which the facts of the question have been set out, specifically enumerating the problems faced by the company's liquidator, is actually a great help to you in organising your answer and you should follow the pattern set.

Skeleton Solution

Function and definition of promoters.

Capacity of company and those acting on its behalf to enter into pre-incorporation contracts.

Application of s36C Companies Act 1985 to such contracts.

Steps a company needs to have taken once incorporated in order to obtain benefit of such contracts.

Equitable and common law duties owed by promoters to company.

Has there in fact been a breach of duty?

Remedies of company against promoters.

Suggested Solution

The liquidator of Joint Engineering Ventures is faced with two sets of legal problems. Firstly, can he, on behalf of the insolvent company, claim the benefit of those contracts entered into purportedly on its behalf prior to its formation (for a company only exists from the date shown in the certificate of incorporation: s13(3) Companies Act (CA) 1985)? Secondly does the company have any remedies against Jane, Henry and Isobel which would swell the pool of assets available for the company's creditors, and do Jane, Henry and Isobel have any valid claims against the company?

The general position with pre-incorporation contracts is that a company cannot ratify and adopt a contract made on its behalf before it was formed since it was not legally in existence when the contract was made. Instead, in order for the company to obtain the benefit of the contract there must be a novation, ie a new contract must be made on the same terms as the old one with the company as a party: *Natal Land and Colonization Co Ltd* v *Pauline Colliery and Development Syndicate* (1). Hence Regulation 51 of the articles of Joint Engineering Ventures is not in itself enough to enable the company to assume the obligations mentioned therein. The answer to the liquidator's first problem (a) then is that since no other steps were taken to transfer the lease assumed by Henry the company is not subject to any obligations under it neither does it enjoy any rights under it. Henry, however, is still personally liable under the lease despite the 'understanding' of a subsequent transfer to the company. There is no evidence that the contrary agreement envisaged by s36C CA 1985, which would absolve him from personal liability, is present.

The second problem the liquidator faces is Henry's claim for the £5,000 deposit he paid on the lease. When Henry paid out those monies the company did not exist so there is no possibility of a contractual obligation for the company to repay him arising at that time. He may try and argue he has a right of indemnity by the company for his out of pocket expenses incurred during his promotion of the company (for Henry was a promoter of the company prior to its formation – see later discussion of promoters). However, there is no such general right either, contractual or equitable. The best that Henry could hope for is a power in the company's articles that the directors can indemnify promoters' expenses, but this is not a legal obligation, and it is highly unlikely that the liquidator would exercise such a power.

The third problem faced by the liquidator is Jane's seemingly very high claim for legal fees in acting as solicitor to the company during its formation. It is important here to consider exactly in what capacity Jane did act and what that claim for legal fees relates to in terms of the activities she undertook. It appears here that Jane has taken on additional responsibilities and acted as a promoter of the company as well as its solicitor. Normally someone who acts in a merely professional capacity in a company's formation, such as a solicitor registering a company, is not a promoter (s67(3) CA 1985). However, Jane has gone beyond the scope of her professional role and fulfilled functions analogous to a director – arranging and advising on financing and the acquisition of stock. This makes her fall within the judicially developed definition of a promoter of a company which Cockburn CJ described as one who undertakes to form a company with reference to a given project and to get it going and who takes the necessary steps to accomplish that purpose: *Twycross* v *Grant* (2). It is by no means necessary for a promoter subsequently to be a director or member of the company once formed. The liquidator of the company should see off Jane's high bill for 'legal fees' by asking for it to be broken down according to work done. He will see that most of it relates to her promotion activities (no simple company formation costs £7,500!) and the same points made above about promoters' rights to remuneration and expenses apply again. As for that element of the bill that does relate properly to legal work there can be no contractual obligation on the company to pay Jane unless it assumed such an obligation after its formation. Jane received her professional instructions from Henry and Isobel and it is against them she should proceed. Regulation 51 has no effect without proper novation (see above).

Promoters owe fiduciary obligations similar to those owed by an agent and an important element to these duties is that a promoter must not make any secret profit out of the promotion without the company's consent: *Whaley Bridge Calico Printing Co* v *Green* (3). The fourth problem faced by the liquidator is that Jane appears to have breached the fiduciary duty she owes as a promoter of the company in accepting and retaining the £1,500 commission from Kevin on his sale to Henry and Isobel of computer equipment to the company. She did not disclose this commission to Henry and Isobel or the company (once it was formed) and so she cannot argue she has the appropriate independent consent of the company to retaining this commission: *Erlanger* v *New Sombrero Phosphate Company* (4). The liquidator may therefore bring proceedings against Jane to recover this sum.

The liquidator is next faced with finding a remedy which will compensate the company for the loss caused by Jane's procurement of the significantly more expensive financing facilities from Easy Loans. She arranged these as part of her promotion of the company and so the question becomes – Do promoters owe any common law duties of due skill and care in the discharge of their function? If so does Jane's action here put her in breach of that duty and render her liable to compensate the company in damages? There is no evidence that Jane is guilty of deception or fraud in connection with this financing (we are not told she has any connection with Easy Loans) so assuming she is guilty of, at the most, negligence alone then it is not at all clear that Jane will be liable in damages. There is little determinative caselaw here since the judicial discussion of a promoter's common law duties involves cases where there has also been a clear breach of fiduciary duty by promoters. Just as the courts are reluctant to delimit a strict negligence standard for company directors, so too it is likely they would show the same reluctance when it comes to setting high standards of skill and care in promotion.

Finally, the liquidator will be keen to see the increase in value of the engineering equipment bought from Engineering Equipment Ltd innure to the company and not Henry and Isobel personally (there appears to be a mistake in the question in the second paragraph – it is most likely to read 'Henry and *Isobel* as purchasers for ... [etc]'). Engineering Equipment Ltd will not be able to repossess their equipment having delivered it before the liquidation commenced, but will rank with the other unsecured creditors (they do not appear to have any security or valid retention of title arrangement) for payment of the £7,500 purchase price. Can Henry and Isobel claim to be personally entitled to the equipment? Although they might try the ingenious argument that they are so entitled, on the basis that s36C CA 1985 renders them personally liable on this contract, so they ought logically to be able to claim the personal benefit of it but this is unlikely to succeed. Instead a court would apply the fiduciary duty owed by Henry and Isobel as promoters to the company and since they bought this property in their fiduciary capacity as promoters then they are liable to account for any increase in its value to the company under normal fiduciary principles.

References

(1) [1904] AC 103
(2) (1877) CPD 469
(3) (1880) 5 QBD 109
(4) (1878) 3 App Cas 1218

QUESTION 7

General Comment

This question is about separate corporate legal personality and its exceptions and ramifications. Any serious student of company law must have considered the topic, and ought not to have had difficulty in obtaining at least a fairly good mark.

Skeleton Solution

Separate personality of a company.

Exceptions.

Illustrative cases.

Suggested Solution

An incorporated company is in law an entirely distinct and separate legal person from its members. In *Salomon* v *Salomon and Co Ltd* (1) Mr Salomon, who had previously carried on a boot and shoe business as an individual, caused a company to be incorporated and became the holder of almost all of its shares. He then sold and transferred his business to the company and took a secured debenture on its assets for the unpaid balance of the purchase price. When the company became insolvent, the House of Lords held that Mr Salomon, as a secured creditor, had a prior claim to the assets to the claims of the company's unsecured creditors; as distinct legal persons Mr Salomon and the company could trade with each other notwithstanding Mr Salomon's control of the company.

Lee v *Lee's Air Farming Ltd* (2), or analogous cases could also be cited and discussed with advantage.

The *Salomon* principle will equally well apply to Health Industries plc and its two wholly owned subsidiaries; each company is a distinct legal person.

Nevertheless, there are circumstances in which the courts will not apply the doctrine of corporate personality distinct from that of membership. An illustrative case is *Gilford Motor Co Ltd* v *Horne* (3) where the court refused to allow an individual who was bound by a valid restrictive covenant to evade performance by forming a company, with himself as its only substantial shareholder, which would proceed to break the covenant. How wide are the circumstances, apart from fraud, in which the courts will disapply the *Salomon* principle is unclear.

As regards the expropriation of land owned by Property Ltd, it is clear that Property Ltd, which is not a trader, has not lost any profits thereby. But if Health Industries plc and Property Ltd were to be regarded in this context as a single entity, a loss of profit would be incurred. There are two contrasting cases on this point and in the context of similar facts to these of our problem. In *DHN Food Distributors Ltd* v *Tower Hamlets* (4) the Court of Appeal allowed the holding company to claim compensation for disturbance to the business which it carried out on land compulsorily to be acquired from its wholly owned subsidiary. But in *Woolfson* v *Strathclyde Regional Council* (5) the court declined to allow a claim where the circumstances were in many respects similar save that there the company which ran the business did not control the owners of the land. *Woolfson*'s case casts some doubt upon the *Tower Hamlets'* decision; nevertheless it is submitted that, unless and until it is overruled, the *Tower Hamlets'* ruling governs this part of the problem, and might possibly even be extended by analogy to other circumstances such as the liability of Health Industries for the negligently conducted activities of the wholly owned subsidiary Testing Ltd. Alternatively it may be possible to show that the subsidiary was acting as the agent of the parent company, as was found to be the case in *Smith, Stone and Knight* v *Birmingham Corporation* (6). (This, if established, would be another ground for claiming loss of profit from the land acquisition.) The relevant factors listed in *Smith*'s case cannot be easily applied to our problem, since in *Smith*'s case each company was carrying on a business and naturally the judgment was directed to that situation.

Finally, it may be mentioned that a director is not, as such, liable for torts committed by the company of which he is a director; he would be liable if he authorised the tort or personally took part in controlling it. It does not appear that Larry Lincoln has done either of these things.

References

(1)   [1897] AC 11
(2)   [1961] AC 12
(3)   [1933] Ch 935
(4)   [1976] 3 All ER 462
(5)   1978 SLT 159
(6)   [1939] 4 All ER 116

QUESTION 8

General Comment

A question involving the position of minority shareholders is always a strong candidate for inclusion in the paper. Whether the question is set in the guise of to what extent the majority can lawfully make life uncomfortable for the minority, or advising the minority how fair the position is, the basic legal material requiring discussion is still the same.

Skeleton Solution

Division of share capital.
Votes and resolutions.
Clause in articles.
Alterability of articles.
Restraints on alterability.
Terms of contract for sale of business.
Possible claim for breach of contract.
Class rights.
Variation of class rights.

Suggested Solution

Alan holds one quarter of the issued shares and the other directors between them hold over 60 per cent and the remaining shareholders will vote as instructed by Barry. Hence (assuming each share holds only one vote as appears to be the case) the other directors will not only be able to carry a resolution voted on by a show of hands at a general meeting but can also do so on a poll (where there is one vote per share held), which Alan as holder of one tenth of the voting rights would, under Companies Act s373, be able to demand. An ordinary resolution will suffice (subject to the power of veto) to authorise the purchase.

Moreover a resolution to acquire the site could instead be passed at a meeting of the board of directors, where Alan is a minority. Despite the resolutions Alan would as a holder of more than 20 per cent of the shares exercise his veto under the articles;

the veto is effective despite a resolution passed in general meeting approving the acquisition: *Quin and Axtens* v *Salmon* (1).

The other directors may seek to be able to alter the articles and delete the veto by special resolution in general meeting under s5. They (plus the small shareholders who would support them) command the 75 per cent of the votes which is the minimum necessary for its passing (see s378). At least 21 days' notice specifying the intention to propose the resolution as a special resolution must first have been given to the members. Neither waiver of notice nor written resolution procedure are plausible here.

There are, however, certain constraints upon a company's ability to alter its articles. The most relevant is that the alteration must not constitute a fraud on the minority and must be bona fide intended to benefit the company as a whole, if these facts are satisfied the fact that the alteration is productive of hardship to the minority appears to be unimportant: *Allen* v *Gold Reefs of West Africa Ltd* (2). 'Intended to benefit the company as a whole' seems here to relate to the intended benefit of the shareholders as a collective body: *Greenhalgh* v *Arderne Cinemas Ltd* (3). Since there appears to be no evidence of malice towards Alan or that the majority are acting other than in the general interest as they see matters nor that their view is clearly quite unreasonable, the resolution should be valid.

We are not, however, informed of the precise terms of the contract for sale of Alan's business; did the contract itself provide that Alan, as any shareholder with at least 20 per cent of the shares, should have the right of veto? If so, mere alteration of the articles would not of itself be effective to eliminate a right contained in a contract itself quite separate from the articles. In *Bailey* v *British Equitable Assurance Co* (4) the Court of Appeal stated that it would be dangerous to hold that a company had any greater power to breach contracts than a private individual would have. But what remedies can successfully be invoked to protect the contract right seems an uncertain matter. In *British Murac Syndicate* v *Alperton Rubber Co* (5) the court granted an injunction to restrain the company from altering its articles to insert provisions inconsistent with the separate contract, while in *Punt* v *Symons and Co* (6) it was suggested that it might be appropriate to enjoin the company from breaking the separate contract rather than from altering its articles. Or the remedy might be damages only, a position seemingly supported by a dictum of Lord Porter in *Southern Foundries* v *Shirlaw* (7).

It could further be argued that since the rights of each holder of 20 per cent or more of the shares are, under the present articles, different from each shareholder with less than that quantity, and thus constitute a separate class of shares. In *Cumbrian Newspapers Group Ltd v Cumberland and Westmorland Herald Newspaper and Printing Co Ltd* (8) it was held that rights conferred on a shareholder as such by the company's constitution are class rights even though not attached to any particular class of shares. This, if correct, would appear to be the case here. If so, it is suggested that it is far from clear that the variation of class rights provisions in s125 would apply, since these refer to variations where the rights attach to a class of shares. But if s125 did apply, the right conferred by s127 on a holder of at least 15 per cent of the shares to apply to the court within 21 days to disallow a variation, concluded under s125(2) on being satisfied that the variation would be unfairly prejudicial, would also apply; such a plea would, however, be very likely to fail on the merits.

References
(1)   [1909] AC 442
(2)   [1900] 1 Ch 656
(3)   [1951] Ch 286
(4)   [1904] 1 Ch 374
(5)   [1915] 2 Ch 186
(6)   [1903] 2 Ch 506
(7)   [1940] AC 701
(8)   [1986] 3 WLR 26

UNIVERSITY OF LONDON
LLB EXAMINATION 1993
for External Students
PART II EXAMINATION (Scheme A) and THIRD AND FOURTH YEAR EXAMINATIONS (Scheme B)

COMPANY LAW

Tuesday, 8 June: 2.30 pm to 5.30 pm

Answer *FOUR* of the following EIGHT questions, including at least ONE from PART A and at least TWO from PART B.

PART A

1 'In our view the cases ... show ... that the court will use its powers to pierce the corporate veil if it is necessary to achieve justice irrespective of the legal efficacy of the corporate structure under consideration.' Per Cumming-Bruce LJ in *Re a Company* (1985).
   Discuss.

2 'The effect of our entry into the EEC has had, and will continue to have, an almost entirely malign effect on the overall development of English company law.'
   Discuss.

3 'The underlying principle of equity is that a person who acts as a representative of another is in a conflict of interest situation if, either at the time when he accepts appointment or subsequently while he acts as a representative, there is a material interest of his own or of a third person for whom he also acts, and the pursuit or protection of that interest could create a substantial risk that he may not act in the best way to pursue or protect the interest of the person he represents.' (Pennington)
   To what extent, if at all, is this principle relevant in company law at the present day?

PART B

4   Lorry Ltd is operating a road haulage business. It has an issued share capital of 900 £1 shares. Alan, Barry and Colin own 300 shares each. The articles of association of the company provide that, 'Alan, Barry and Colin are to be the directors of the company and each is to receive a salary of £25,000 per annum.'

The company was formed in 1987 and was immediately successful. Every year Alan, Barry and Colin have each drawn £25,000. No dividends have been paid on their shares but the huge profits of the company have been ploughed back into the business, so that now each £1 share is represented by assets worth about £1,000, and thus the total asset value of the company is about £900,000.

In 1990 Colin quarrelled with Alan and Barry over matters of business policy. After that, they made it difficult for Colin to have any real share in the management of the business because, although they still had regular weekly directors' meetings at which they were all present, Alan and Barry discussed and made all the business decisions in advance and invariably outvoted Colin at the board meetings. At first Colin complained bitterly about this, but after some months he lost all interest in the business and has not now attended a board meeting for nearly two years.

In recent months Colin has suspected that Alan and Barry have been diverting the company's haulage contracts to a newly formed company registered with the name Lorry (London) Ltd of which Alan and Barry are the sole shareholders and directors. Last week Colin confronted Alan and Barry with this and there was a violent quarrel. They have just written to him informing him that he is 'sacked as director and will receive no more salary from the company'.

Advise Colin.

5   In 1986, Helen, then aged 24, qualified as a chartered accountant. In 1987 she formed Pear Ltd and its wholly-owned subsidiary, Sub Ltd. Helen holds all the shares in Pear Ltd except one, which is held by a nominee for her. Pear Ltd holds all the shares in Sub Ltd, except one, which is similarly held by a nominee for Pear Ltd. Helen is the only director of both companies and neither company has filed any accounts with the Registrar for the last three years. Other than her shares in Pear Ltd, Helen has virtually no assets.

Since 1987 Pear Ltd has made telephone answering machines and has flourished so that it now has assets of over £1 million and employs 40 people. Sub Ltd however, is mainly engaged in supplying Pear Ltd with components and is not run primarily with a view to making a profit on its own, although for the first two years, 1988 and 1989, Sub Ltd made profits of £8,000 and £3,000 respectively. However in 1990 it made a loss of £38,000; in 1991 a loss of £23,000 and in 1992 a loss of £11,000.

In September 1991 Big Bank plc was pressing for a reduction of Sub Ltd's overdraft of £40,000. Helen then paid £20,000 of her own money into the account, taking in return a debenture from Sub Ltd for £20,000 and a floating charge to secure both that £20,000 and an earlier loan by her to the company of £15,000.

On 2 April 1993 a creditor presented a petition for the winding up of Sub Ltd and a winding up order was made on 14 May 1993. The assets of Sub Ltd fall short of its liabilities by £60,000.

Advise Helen as to her potential liabilities, if any, and her position generally.

6 The objects clause of the memorandum of association of Southerly Breezes Ltd contains only the following:
   i) The objects of the company are to manufacture and sell sailing yachts.
   ii) The company shall have power to do any act which is incidental or conducive to the attainment of the above objects.

The company is currently successfully engaged in its business of making and selling sailing yachts. Emily and Roland are the directors of the company but own no shares in it. In 1991 they were approached by Gina, a close friend of Roland, who was seeking a guarantee of a loan of £100,000 which she was negotiating with Spartan Bank plc. The directors said 'a friend in need is a friend indeed' and, having sent a copy of the memorandum of the company to the bank, caused the company to give a guarantee to the bank in respect of the £100,000.

In March 1993 Gina was made bankrupt and the bank commenced an action against the company on the guarantee. In May 1993 a specially convened meeting of the shareholders of the company passed the following resolutions by 51 per cent majority vote:

a) Ratifying the directors' actions in giving the guarantee and authorising payment under it.

b) Authorising a donation of £25,000 to the general funds of the Green Party.

Harvey, who is holder of 49 per cent of the shares, voted against the resolutions at the meeting. Advise him as to whether there are any legal grounds for getting the resolutions set aside.

7 Ox Ltd was formed in 1986 and carries on a business manufacturing nuts and bolts. The memorandum of association provides, inter alia, that the share capital of the company is divided into 50,000 £1 ordinary shares and 10,000 £1 preference shares. Further, the preference shares are there expressed to carry rights to a 16 per cent preference dividend. All the share capital has been issued.

In 1989, after lengthy negotiations, Ox Ltd purchased a factory from Pin Ltd, a company which has owned 5,000 of the ordinary shares in Ox Ltd since its formation in 1986. As part of the consideration for the purchase, it was agreed that the articles of association of Ox Ltd would be altered so as to give Pin Ltd special pre-emption rights in the event of other members of Ox Ltd wishing to sell their shares. The alteration of articles was carried out by Ox Ltd early in 1990.

The board of directors of Ox Ltd now wish to remove from the articles the rights of Pin Ltd in respect of pre-emption, although they are aware that Pin Ltd would oppose this. They also wish to reduce the preference dividend from 16 per cent to 10 per cent. They have heard that 85 per cent of the preference shareholders would be prepared to accede to this reduction since they have all become aware that the company is in financial difficulties and wish to help it. The remaining 15 per cent of the preference shareholders would be opposed to this reduction.

Advise the directors.

8 Robber plc has two wholly owned subsidiaries, Sud Ltd and Tot Ltd. Although all three companies satisfactorily function independently of each other, Robber plc is to some extent reliant on the factories of the subsidiaries for supplies of electronic circuitry for its missile factory.

The board of directors of Tot Ltd have decided that it is virtually essential for Tot Ltd to acquire a more powerful computer system for its factory. Tot Ltd can only afford to raise £150,000 for this, but the system needed, the 'Biggerbyte 601' normally costs around £250,000. The board have recently heard, however, that Ven is prepared to supply the 'Biggerbyte 601' for £180,000, and that Sud Ltd would be prepared to lend £30,000 to Tot Ltd to help with this. Ven holds 15 per cent of the shares in Robber plc and is hoping to use the proceeds of sale of the 'Biggerbyte 601' to acquire a further 3 per cent.

At their board meeting last week, the directors of Tot Ltd decided to go ahead with the purchase of the 'Biggerbyte 601' from Ven, partly because of the low price he is offering and also because they would be happy to see him acquire more shares in Robber plc since they believe that Ven's large stake acts as a deterrent to foreign takeover bidders. The directors of Tot Ltd are anxious to go ahead but have heard that there may be legal problems.

Advise the board of directors of Tot Ltd.

PART A
QUESTION 1

General Comment
A fairly standard question. Students should display a close knowledge and detailed analysis of the cases where there have been attempts to lift the veil. To score well, candidates should go further than merely listing the authorities and citing their diversity as evidence of a lack of any consistent approach.

Skeleton Solution
A matter of substance or form – the one man company.

Lifting the veil – a single economic entity – a sham or facade and legitimate group structures – implied agency.

Fraud – the courts' discretion.

Suggested Solution
That the authorities are not unified by any clearly discernible principle (other than in clear cases of fraud) might be attributable to a dilemma striking at the very foundation of company law. Is the veil of incorporation truly a 'veil', ie a matter of form rather than substance? If the answer is yes then there will frequently be strong reasons why the veil ought to be lifted in order to look at the underlying reality. If the answer is no, then the court should have a clear foundation in law for disregarding a matter of substance.

The quotation given in the question would, if correct, enable the court to draw aside the veil at will if it were necessary to achieve a desirable goal, eg to find in favour of a meritorious litigant who did not appreciate or understand the significance of incorporation. This cannot be correct. That incorporation effects a fundamental change of substance and not form is beyond doubt following the House of Lords decision in *Salomon* v *Salomon & Co Ltd* (1). Even a 'one man' company has an existence independent of its members: *Lee* v *Lee's Air Farming Ltd* (2). Thus the veil ought to be pierced only exceptionally and on a clear basis in law. The principle enunciated by Cumming Bruce LJ could not therefore provide a foundation for piercing the veil and was in fact decisively rejected by the Court of Appeal in *Adams v Cape Industries Plc* (3).

The principal issue in this case was whether Cape (the parent of NAAC which faced personal injuries claims in the United States) had via its subsidiary been present in and was therefore bound by a judgment obtained in the United States. The plaintiffs attempted to contend that Cape had been present in the United States for three reasons: firstly, because Cape and its subsidiary should be treated as a single economic entity as per *DHN Food Distributors Ltd v Tower Hamlets LBC* (4); secondly, because the corporate veil of Cape ought not to shield it from liability; and thirdly because Cape was liable as principal for NAAC. The Court of Appeal held that: Cape and NAAC ought not to be treated as a single economic entity for present purposes which test was to be largely confined to cases where the issue was one of construction of a document or statute; that the veil could not be lifted on the basis that the corporate structure was a facade as per *Jones v Lipman* (5) because there was nothing objectionable in a group adopting a particular structure in order to ensure that potential liabilities fell upon one company rather than another; and finally that there was on the facts no actual agency and there could never be a presumed agency merely by virtue of the relationship of principal and subsidiary.

The Court of Appeal has therefore injected some clarity into this area. But noticeably the court did not give any guidance as to when a company ought to be treated as a facade, eg solely in cases of fraud. Fraud will undoubtedly suffice as per the numerous authorities, especially *Gilford Motor Co v Horne* (6) and *Re Darby, ex parte Brougham* (7). What however where there is no fraud as in *Re FG (Films) Ltd* (8)? In this case Vaisey J found as a matter of fact that an agency existed between the parent and subsidiary and possibly therefore the case ought to be regarded as one of simple agency rather than lifting the veil in the proper sense.

In conclusion it might be said that there are now some albeit sparse guide-lines as to when the court will be prepared to pierce the veil, in particular where incorporation is used as a facade or sham arrangement. Whilst it is difficult in cases other than fraud to discern when a company will be treated as a sham it is arguable that this provides for a greater flexibility and therefore a greater range of application. What is clear is that the courts do not have an unfettered discretion to pierce the veil irrespective of the legal efficacy of the corporate structure under consideration.

References

(1) [1897] AC 22
(2) [1961] AC 12
(3) [1991] 1 All ER 929
(4) [1976] 1 WLR 852
(5) [1962] 1 WLR 832
(6) [1933] Ch 935
(7) [1911] 1 KB 95
(8) [1953] 1 WLR 483

QUESTION 2

General Comment

A fairly simple question provided that the candidate has a sufficient working knowledge of the underlying subject matter. A good opportunity for candidates to illustrate that they have their finger on the pulse.

Skeleton Solution

Impact of Community law upon UK company law – aims of secondary legislation – difficulties.

Examples of secondary legislation translated into Companies Acts – are the difficulties with the implementation conceptual or practical? – has the UK achieved the aims of the secondary legislation?

The future – proposals for increased worker participation – a supervisory board for the plc.

Suggested Solution

That Community law has already had a tremendous impact on English company law cannot be doubted. To maintain that its effect upon English company law is and will continue to be entirely malign is demonstrably inaccurate. Such inadequacies as have appeared to date may be properly attributed to our own parliamentary draftsmen who experience difficulties in expressing secondary legislation in terms appropriate to the domestic canvas. Hence many Community reforms were introduced in CA 1985, but have only recently been properly implemented 'second time around' by virtue of CA 1989. That the problems are not conceptual is best illustrated by considering some of the principal (and almost entirely beneficial) changes that have been made to our domestic law.

Perhaps the most significant changes to domestic law can be seen in the form of the new ss35, 35A, 35B as implemented by s108 CA 1989. In its original unamended form s35 CA 1985 represented the codification of Article 9 of the First Directive on Company Law of 1968. Its greatest flaw was that s35 attempted to deal in an instant with the doctrine of ultra vires but without distinguishing between ultra vires and directors' want of authority. This and the wording of the section itself led to difficulties of interpretation, for example, when does a person 'deal' with a company? What was meant by 'good faith'? Did the transaction have to be expressly approved by all of the directors? Lawson J's judgment in *International Sales Agencies Ltd v Marcus* (1) is famous for providing answers to some at least of these questions. But it is more significant for present purposes to note that the directive itself made no mention of 'dealing' or 'good faith'. These constructions were the product of our own draftsmen. Thus the fault lay not with the aim of the Commission but with our implementation of the directive.

These problems were largely ironed out by s108 CA 1989 which noticeably avoids any reference to 'dealing' and provides guidance as to the meaning of 'good faith'.

The beneficial effects of Community intervention may also be seen in the area of consolidated accounts and in particular the obligations imposed by virtue of the Seventh Directive (Pt VII and Sched 4A CA 1985). By virtue of these amendments there is a new (and more stringent) definition of parent and subsidiary and there is also an obligation on companies to include unincorporated subsidiary 'undertakings' (eg, partnerships) owned by the group in the accounts. The value of this practice is that companies are now less likely to be able to borrow massive amounts via subsidiaries but to keep the subsidiary and therefore also the subsidiary's borrowing off the group balance sheet. The effect is entirely beneficial since the investing public is less likely to be misled into investing in a group that appears to be more solvent than it in fact is.

The above directives represent a fraction of the law that has passed into our statute books in the area of company law. If there is to be a complaint about the impact of Community law then it must be largely centred around the piecemeal approach of the Commission to reform. Thus as directives are issued the national states make legislation without knowing (with any certainty) whether a further directive will require alteration of the legislation based upon the preceding directive.

Before concluding we must ask whether there are likely to be any future malign consequences of our membership of the EEC. Again, because of the piecemeal approach (referred to above) little more can be done than to consider briefly some of the proposed changes that may or may not become law.

Two notable changes may be found in the draft Fifth Directive.

Firstly it provides for more effective monitoring of management in the case of plcs by making a division between directors responsible for management and those responsible for their supervision. Especially significant is the proposal that directors are to be jointly and severally liable except to the extent that the individual director can prove that no fault is personally attributable to him. If implemented such a proposal can only serve to better managerial standards and hopefully go some way towards preventing the reoccurrence of commercial catastrophes like the Maxwell and/or Polly Peck sagas.

Secondly, the Fifth Directive contains proposals to increase worker participation, possibly by guaranteed representation at board level. The precise degree of participation afforded to workers is a matter for debate, but it cannot be doubted but that an informed and well represented workforce is likely to be more productive. This last proposal may however be significantly at odds with the government policy of some member states and depending on political viewpoint may be a malign prospect. In the final analysis however, our entry into the EEC must be seen on balance to have had and be likely to have overwhelmingly beneficial consequences.

Reference
(1)   [1982] 3 All ER 551

QUESTION 3

General Comment
It is usual to find a question requiring the candidate to illustrate an understanding of the fiduciary duties owed by directors and this is it. To achieve a good score the candidate should have a detailed understanding of the principal authorities.

Skeleton Solution
Two limbs of fiduciary duty – no profit and no conflict rules – circumvention.

Fiduciary duty to account – irrelevance of mala fides – irrelevance of whether or not at company's expense.

Distinction between ratifiable and non-ratifiable conduct – fraud on the minority – judicial inroads – consideration of circumstances in which profit made – an equitable allowance.

Suggested Solution
The quotation provides an exposition of the rule that a fiduciary must not place himself in a position where his duty and interest conflict ('the no conflict rule'). Nor must he profit by virtue of his position ('the no profit rule'). Transgression of either rule has serious consequences for the fiduciary who will be liable to account to the company for any breach. The logic underpinning the no conflict and no profit rules is readily understandable. Less readily understandable are the sometimes perverse and more importantly harsh results occasioned by a strict application of the rules: *Regal (Hastings) Ltd* v *Gulliver* (1). An examination of the authorities displays a hitherto tendency on behalf of the courts to hold the fiduciary liable to account regardless of his moral culpability, although it is arguable that recent inroads have been made.

Dealing firstly with the no conflict rule, its significance rests more in theory than practice. Contracts with the company are voidable at the instance of the company: *Aberdeen Railway Co* v *Blaikie Bros* (2). It is significant that the court will not inquire into the fairness of the transaction. Nor will the court require to be satisfied that there is an actual conflict of duty and interest. It is sufficient if there is a real possibility of conflict *Phipps* v *Boardman* (3). Where the rule is transgressed the company may nevertheless in general meeting vote to ratify the contract.

It will be immediately apparent that there are often situations where for example a director may be able to supply goods or services to a company in a way that is especially advantageous to the company financially. In such cases the process of convening a general meeting solely for the purpose of approving that each contract would be administratively burdensome. Article 85 and 86 therefore of the current Table A permit directors to be interested in contracts with the company provided that those interests are disclosed to the remaining directors.

Where the articles of the company embody such a provision strict adherence to it is paramount: *Guiness plc* v *Saunders* (4). In this case the House of Lords took the opportunity to reaffirm the proposition that a fiduciary must not place himself in a position where his duty and interest conflict. However, Lord Goff went on to point out that in exceptional circumstances the court might make an equitable allowance in favour of the director on the basis of a quantum meruit. Further that such an allowance would be available where it did not encourage other directors to transgress the rule. It will be seen therefore that the no conflict rule is not an insurmountable obstacle to either directors or companies. Where however it is sought to legitimately circumnavigate the rule, the director must be attentive to the procedure laid down in the company's articles.

More problematic is the difficulty posed by the no profit rule as it relates to the use or misuse of corporate opportunity or information. In *Regal* (supra) the House of Lords held enterprising directors liable to account, notwithstanding that the profit made by them was not at the expense of the company. The motives of the directors were irrelevant to the question of liability which was based on a strict application of the doctrine in *Keech* v *Sandford* (5). Significantly however their Lordships pointed out that the directors might have protected themselves by resolution of the company in general meeting. On the basis of *Regal* alone it would have been possible for any director (particularly in the case of small or quasi-partnership companies) to ensure that a resolution was passed ratifying the breach of the no profit rule.

Whether or not ratification is always possible is not free from doubt. Thus in *Cook* v *Deeks* (6) the Privy Council decided that the directors' purported ratification of their profit (voting qua members) was tantamount to a gift to themselves of corporate property. The rationale of their Lordships was that the opportunity for profit belonged at all times in equity to the company as a result of which it was not open to the directors to deal with it other than for the benefit of the company. Hence it is important but extremely difficult for any director wishing to profit to know whether or not his conduct is ratifiable. Where it is not the director might be the defendant to a derivative action by a member on behalf of the company. Arguably the distinction lies in those cases where the profit is incidental to a transaction that is of benefit to the company as opposed to those cases where profit for the directors is the primary aim of the transaction.

Recent authority has however indicated a willingness on behalf of the courts to allow the fiduciary to retain profits or opportunities where the same are not acquired at the expense of the company. In particular in *Canadian Aero Services Ltd v O'Malley* (7) and *Island Export Finance Ltd v Umuna* (8) the courts started to consider the circumstances in which the profit was made, a fairly radical departure from a strict application of the no profit rule.

In conclusion the resulting position would appear to be thus. The fiduciary duty of the director continues to be relevant to company law today although it will be frequently possible for directors to protect themselves from its bite. This is especially so in the case of small companies where the directors are also likely to hold a majority of votes. It will however always be a counsel of prudence for any director to take sound legal advice before contemplating any breach of duty. A resolution purporting to ratify the breach of duty might provide cold comfort where the act is not ratifiable.

References

(1) [1942] 1 All ER 378
(2) (1854) 1 Macq 461
(3) [1964] 1 WLR 993
(4) [1990] 2 AC 663
(5) (1726) Sel Cas Ch 21
(6) [1916] AC 554
(7) (1973) 40 DLR 371
(8) [1986] BCLC 460

PART B
QUESTION 4

General Comment
An eye for the salient facts and an appreciation of the limits of the remedies available are required.

Skeleton Solution
The s14 contract – 'outsider rights' – contracts extrinsic but identical to the articles.
Shareholder remedies – s459 CA 1985 – s122 IA 1986 and limitations thereon – interrelation between derivative action and s459.

Suggested Solution
Colin has a plethora of remedies available to him. There are three main issues: (1) does Colin have a contractual remedy against Lorry Ltd on the basis of a contract contained in the articles?; (2) is exclusion from the board actionable qua member?; and (3) can Colin pursue any remedy against Alan and Barry on behalf of Lorry Ltd?

1) Section 14 CA 1985 gives contractual effect to the memorandum and articles between the members inter se, and between the members and the company. The effect is that every member has a contractual right to enforce observance of the articles: *Wood* v *Odessa Waterworks Co* (1). There are however important restrictions on the type of right which may be enforced. Most significantly the rights enforceable are only those which affect the member in his capacity as member: *Eley* v *Positive Government Security Life Assurance Co Ltd* (2). In the instant case the relevant article provides that Colin is to be director. The right is therefore not conferred qua shareholder and prima facie Colin has no action on the basis of the contract contained in the articles.

   There are however two further possibilities. The first is that Colin may be able to bring an action qua member to have the articles enforced (the fact that this will result in his being reinstated as a director being incidental to the action). There is no direct authority in Colin's favour in point although the House of Lords in *Quin & Axtens* v *Salmon* (3) upheld the plaintiff's injunction qua member although it affected him principally qua director. The second possibility is that the court would be prepared to imply a contract extrinsic but identical to the articles, alterable unilaterally by the company: *Re New British Iron Co, ex parte Beckwith* (4). On this basis Colin would at least be able to recover any arrears of salary.

2) As a shareholder Colin has potentially at his disposal two important remedies. He may petition the court for a just and equitable winding up of Lorry Ltd pursuant to s122(g) IA 1986. Alternatively he may bring proceedings under s459 CA 1985 for unfairly prejudicial conduct. Frequently the same set of facts will give rise to the availability of either remedy. Exclusion from participation in management was recognised as a ground for just and equitable winding up (at least in relation to quasi-partnership companies) by the House of Lords in *Ebrahimi* v *Westbourne Galleries Ltd* (5). As a condition precedent to granting relief the court will require to be satisfied as to the existence of one or more of the following criteria: (a) the company should have been formed on the basis of a personal relationship involving mutual trust and confidence; (b) there should be some agreement that all or some of the shareholders participate in the management of the business; and (c) there should be pre-emption rights over the shares. The crux of the matter is that the court will not intervene unless the agreement embodied in the articles does not properly define the parties' rights and expectations.

Colin is attempting to invoke an equitable jurisdiction and so the court will be interested in whether or not he has 'clean hands' and has delayed in seeking this remedy. Colin should also bear in mind that to have the company wound up will be to 'kill the goose that lays the golden eggs'. In view of the fact that the value of the company has increased from £900 in 1987 to £900,000 at the present day, Colin would be advised to view this remedy as a last resort.

By virtue of s461 the court has an almost unlimited discretion as to the appropriate order upon the hearing of a petition under s459 alleging unfairly prejudicial conduct. Commonly the order will be that petitioners' shares be purchased by the respondent. The range of remedies available should alone make this a more attractive choice of remedy to Colin. The paramount question is whether there has been any unfair prejudice.

In common with the remedy of the just and equitable winding up, exclusion from management can form the basis of an unfair prejudice application: *Re London School of Electronics Ltd* (6). As before the court will require to be satisfied that the removal from the board is both unfair and prejudicial. Mere removal alone will not suffice and so much depends on the basis upon which Colin became a member of Lorry Ltd. There is no requirement that Colin come to the court with clean hands although his non attendance at board meetings may influence the court as to the relief which it is prepared to grant. There is however one further element which may make a petition under s459 the most appropriate remedy.

3) Can Colin pursue any remedy against Alan and Barry for allegedly diverting contracts to the newly formed Lorry (London) Ltd? According to the rule in *Foss* v *Harbottle* (7) the proper plaintiff in an action in this respect would be Lorry Ltd. As malefactors and majority shareholders Barry and Alan are unlikely to procure Lorry Ltd to bring proceedings against themselves. Prima facie therefore there is a fraud on the minority of exactly the type contemplated in *Cooks* v *Deeks* (8) which Colin may attempt to redress on behalf of Lorry Ltd in a separate derivative action. It should be noted however that under s459 CA 1985 as amended by CA 1989 conduct which is prejudicial to the interests of the 'members generally' will be actionable. Prior to this amendment conduct which affected all members equally (and therefore in reality the company itself) was not actionable. In the present case Alan and Barry's actions will ultimately diminish the value of theirs and Colin's holdings in Lorry Ltd. It is therefore open to Colin to remedy this loss to Lorry Ltd under s459. It should be noted that by virtue of s461(2)(c) the court may authorise civil proceedings to be brought in the name and on behalf of the company. This would thereby enable Colin to redress wrongs done to both himself and Lorry Ltd in a single petition under s459 by sidestepping the confusing rules governing common law derivative actions.

References

(1) (1889) 42 Ch D 636
(2) (1876) 1 Ex D 88
(3) [1909] AC 442
(4) [1898] 1 Ch 326
(5) [1973] AC 360

References (continued)
(6) [1986] Ch 211
(7) (1843) 2 Have 461
(8) [1916] 1 AC 554

QUESTION 5

General Comment

A fairly straightforward question requiring an understanding of the remedies available to liquidators of insolvent companies.

Skeleton Solution

Avoidance of floating charges – 'connected persons'.

Wrongful trading – parent companies as shadow directors – relevance of Helen's qualification as an accountant.

Company Directors Disqualification Act 1986.

Suggested Solution

The issues are: (1) is the floating charge taken by Helen totally or partially void?; (2) could Helen have incurred liability for wrongful trading?; and (3) is Helen likely to be disqualified as a director?

1) Section 245(2)(a) IA 1986 enables the liquidator of an insolvent company in certain circumstances to avoid floating charges. It provides in essence that a floating charge created at the relevant time will be invalid except to the extent of the aggregate of the fresh consideration supplied to the company at the same time as or after the creation of the charge. The relevant time for the above purposes is defined in s245(3)(a) as being two years in the case of a charge created in favour of a person connected with the company, beginning with the onset of the insolvency.

From the facts of the instant case it can be seen that in September 1991, Helen in return for her cash injection of £20,000 took a debenture secured by a floating charge to the value of £35,000. As a director of Sub Ltd, Helen is a connected person and so the floating charge (since it was created less than two years before the winding up order made in May 1993) is potentially liable to challenge from the liquidator. The question is whether Helen has provided fresh consideration. Section 245 IA 1986 aims to prevent the substitution of a secured debt for an unsecured debt. Provided the payment is for the benefit of the company the court will treat it as fresh consideration, *Re Matthew Ellis Ltd* (1). As per the wording of the statute the consideration provided in return for the charge is £20,000. Helen's security is therefore likely to be valid only to the value of £20,000. She may seek to prove as an ordinary unsecured creditor for the balance of £15,000 but in view of the £60,000 shortfall of assets over liabilities will receive nothing.

2) Is Helen liable for wrongful trading? In order to hold a director liable for wrongful trading the court must be satisfied that at some time before the commencement of the winding up, the director knew or ought to have concluded that there was no reasonable prospect of the company avoiding going into insolvent liquidation: s214 IA 1986. Section 214(4) IA 1986 provides that the facts of which the director will be taken to know will be judged according to: the general knowledge, skill and experience that may reasonably be expected of a person carrying out the same functions of that director, and the general knowledge, skill and experience that that director has. Helen's conduct will therefore be judged according to both objective and subjective standards. It should be noted that the standard is almost certainly therefore higher than that required to be exhibited by directors in the discharge of their common law duties of care and skill: per Romer J in *Re City Equitable Fire Insurance Ltd* (2). It is significant therefore that Helen is a qualified accountant as a consequence of which her decision to continue to trade will be measured against the likely decision of a similarly qualified 'reasonable' accountant.

We are told that Helen has not caused Sub Ltd to produce any annually audited accounts for the last three years. Helen's failure mirrors that of the directors in *Re Produce Marketing Consortium (No 2)* (3). In this case Knox J found that the directors could not rely on their own failure to keep proper accounts as a defence to the contention that they knew or ought to have known that the company would enter an insolvent liquidation. The only defence available to Helen is that once the inevitability of an insolvent liquidation occurred to her, she took every step with a view to minimising loss to creditors that she ought reasonably to have taken: s214(3) IA 1986. Thus far Helen is prima facie liable for wrongful trading.

Helen might seek to take solace in the fact that Pear Ltd whilst the parent of Sub Ltd is a different company and accordingly should logically remain unaffected by the demise of its subsidiary. She should be advised however that liability for wrongful trading applies to 'shadow directors' as it does to formally appointed directors. The term is defined in s251 as 'a person in accordance with whose directions or instructions the directors of the company are accustomed to act'. We are told that Sub Ltd exists mainly for the purpose of supplying Pear Ltd with components. It is not inconceivable (although there is no authority directly in point) that because of the high degree of connection between the two companies, Pear Ltd may be regarded by the court as a shadow director of Sub Ltd. Thus the assets of Pear Ltd may ultimately be used to satisfy the £60,000 shortfall.

3) Is Helen likely to be disqualified as a director pursuant to the CDDA 1986? The 1986 Act provides numerous grounds upon which Helen may be disqualified. By virtue of ss3, 6, and 11 she may be disqualified on the following grounds respectively; for persistent breach of companies legislation (failure to deliver accounts and annual return); duty of court to disqualify unfit directors of insolvent companies; disqualification for participation in wrongful trading. In relation to 'unfitness', Parts I and II of Schedule 1 to the Act list the factors that are to be considered by the court in determining fitness. As to the behaviour warranting disqualification it will require at the very least a lack of commercial probity as opposed to ordinary misjudgment: *Re Lino Electric Motors Ltd* (4).

References

(1) [1933] Ch 458
(2) [1925] Ch 407
(3) [1989] BCLC 520
(4) [1988] 4 Ch 477

QUESTION 6

General Comment

A question requiring the candidate to illustrate a clear understanding of the often confusing areas of ultra vires and directors' want of authority. Those who are able to demonstrate such understanding would be likely to score well on this question.

Skeleton Solution

Construction of objects clause – objects and powers – transactions intra vires but in excess or abuse of directors' authority.

Ratification of directors' actions – ordinary or special majority – s35(3) CA 1985.

Remedies – derivative action – unfairly prejudicial conduct.

Suggested Solution

Harvey's concerns about the resolutions passed at the general meeting in May 1993 are well founded since their effect will be to deprive the company of £125,000.

Dealing firstly with the guarantee given to Spartan Bank Plc, it is first of all necessary to decide whether or not the transaction was ultra vires since this may affect the appropriate majority by which the resolutions were allegedly passed. In *Rolled Steel Products (Holdings) Ltd v British Steel Corporation* (1) the Court of Appeal stated that ultra vires depended on the true construction of the memorandum. Thus any transaction falling within the ambit of an express object would be intra vires unless by its very nature it was incapable of standing as an independent object.

In the instant case the objects of the company are limited to the manufacture and selling of sailing yachts and all things incidental or conducive to the attainment of those objects. It has not been doubted since the House of Lords decision in *A-G v Great Eastern Railway* (2) that a company has every ancillary power reasonably incidental to the express objects. Thus Harvey would not be able to successfully contend that the company could never in any circumstances give guarantees. The difficulty in the instant case is that the guarantee is apparently given for no other purpose than the friendship between Emily, Roland and Gina. Prima facie therefore the guarantee is ultra vires. It must also for the same reason involve an excess of directors' authority.

Under the old common law it had never been competent for a company (even by unanimous consent) to ratify a contract that was ultra vires its objects: *Ashbury Railway Carriage & Iron Co Ltd* v *Riche* (3). By virtue of s35(3) CA 1985 a company may now ratify any ultra vires act by special resolution. By virtue of the same subsection it is also possible to relieve a director from liability for the same. It should be noted however that such relief must be given by the passing of a separate special resolution from that ratifying the ultra vires act. Applying this to the facts of the present case it can be seen that resolution (a) falls foul of s35(3) for the following reasons: firstly, it purports in a single resolution to ratify payment under the guarantee and to relieve Harvey from liability; secondly, it purports to have been passed by a simple majority.

In relation to resolution (a) therefore it is open to Harvey to apply to the court for a declaration that the resolution is invalid. He may also wish to procure the company to take action against Emily and Roland to recover the £100,000 lost by virtue of honouring the guarantee. Although the company is the proper plaintiff, Harvey may well be able to bring himself within the exception to the rule in *Foss* v *Harbottle* (4) which permits the individual to restrain the company from acting on the basis of a resolution which has not been passed by the requisite majority: *Quin Axtens* v *Salmon* (5). If the guarantee had not been ultra vires it would have been open to the company in general meeting to relieve Emily and Roland from liability by ordinary resolution: *Grant* v *United Kingdom Switchbank Rly Co* (6).

Turning to the £25,000 donation to the Green Party, it can be seen at a glance that this payment is entirely gratuitous. The legality of gratuitous payments has been the subject of much judicial and academic debate. In *Hutton* v *West Cork Rly Co* (7) Bowen LJ said that there should be 'no cakes and ale except such as are required for the benefit of the company'. In *Re Lee, Behrens & Co Ltd* (8), Eve J laid down a three stage test in order to determine the validity of corporate gifts. At the 'heart' of the test was the question of whether or not the transaction was reasonably incidental to the carrying on of the company's business. *Behrens* (supra) was doubted subsequently by the Court of Appeal in *Re Horsley & Weight Ltd* (9) where the court held that it was possible for a company to have a charitable purpose as an express substantive object, in which case the 'benefit' test in *Behrens* was irrelevant. In the instant case however the company has no express charitable object as a consequence of which the benefit to the company must be relevant. The donation to the Green Party is therefore ultra vires. If the donation has not already been made then it is open to Harvey to apply for an injunction against Emily and Roland to restrain payment pursuant to s35A(4) CA 1985.

In the event that the £25,000 has already been paid Harvey may seek to bring a derivative action against Emily and Roland to recover this sum. Harvey should also be advised that any derivative action may now be brought under s459 CA 1985 which enables the court to authorise any individual to bring proceedings on behalf of the company: s461(2)(c).

References

(1) [1984] BCLC 466
(2) (1880) 5 App Cas 354
(3) (1875) LR 7 HL 653
(4) (1843) 2 Hare 461
(5) [1909] AC 442
(6) (1888) 40 Ch D 135
(7) (1883) 23 Ch D 654
(8) [1932] 2 Ch 46
(9) [1982] Ch 442

QUESTION 7

General Comment

A question requiring the candidate to look very carefully at the problem. Once the 'perception threshold' of the question is broken the solution is not too difficult. A question likely to be avoided by many candidates and therefore an opportunity for the individual to distinguish himself/herself.

Skeleton Solution

Articles of association – restrictions on alteration – bona fide for the benefit of the company; subjective or objective test.

Ascertainment of class rights – variation of class rights – what alterations constitute a variation?

Rights of dissenting minority.

Suggested Solution

The directors of Ox Ltd ('the company') wish to alter its articles in order to achieve two things: firstly they wish to divest Pin Ltd of the pre-emption rights acquired on its sale of the factory to the company: secondly they wish to reduce the dividend attaching to the preference shares from 16 per cent to 10 per cent. We are told that both Pin Ltd and 15 per cent of the preference shareholders are unlikely to acquiesce to the alterations. There is therefore a possibility that the alterations might be challenged by either of the above groups on the basis that they constitute a variation of a class right necessitating approval by that class alone: and/or that the alterations are not in any event 'bona fide for the benefit of the company'.

Dealing firstly with the alteration removing Pin Ltd's rights of pre-emption, by virtue of s9 CA 1985 any alteration to the articles requires a special resolution. As owner of 20 per cent of the ordinary shares in Ox Ltd, Pin Ltd is prima facie unable to defeat the resolution for alteration. Pin Ltd may however contend that the pre-emption rights currently enjoyed by it are 'class rights' attached to the shares currently held and therefore that any variation will require observance of the procedure for variation laid down in the articles or, alternatively, observance of s125 CA 1985. Are the rights enjoyed by Pin Ltd class rights?

Class rights are more often easier to recognise than to define. Frequently (although not invariably) the rights are expressly defined in the articles. Farrar (*Farrar's Company Law*, 3rd ed p222) states that, 'dissimilar interests alone, not arising from legal rights under the corporate constitution, cannot generally be regarded as sufficient ground for the separation of classes'. There was until recently little authority as to what constitutes a class. A thorough review however was undertaken by Scott J in *Cumbrian Newspaper Group Ltd* v *Cumberland & Westmorland Herald Newspaper and Printing Co Ltd* (1) who adopted a tri-partite classification. Of particular significance to Pin Ltd in the present case is the third category of rights upheld by Scott J in this case. These were rights which although not attached to any particular class of shares were conferred on the beneficiary qua member. In that case the rights were enjoyed on condition that the plaintiff held at least 10.67 per cent of the issued ordinary share capital of the company. Applying this to the facts of the problem it can be seen that the pre-emption rights acquired by Pin Ltd were not referable to (and were unconnected with) its pre-existing membership of the company. They are not therefore rights enjoyed qua member and for that reason neither are they class rights. This alteration at least cannot therefore be a variation of a class right. Thus the only remaining option available to Pin Ltd is to contend that the alteration is not bona fide for the benefit of the company.

The duty of shareholders to vote bona fide in the interests of the company has received a chequered treatment in the authorities over the years. The duty was firmly established by the Court of Appeal in *Allen* v *Gold Reefs of West Africa Ltd* (2). The principal difficulty lies in knowing whether the test is to be applied according to the subjective view of the members or an objective view.

In *Shuttleworth* v *Cox Bros & Co (Maidenhead) Ltd* (3), the Court of Appeal preferred not to interfere where there were grounds on which a reasonable shareholder would come to the same conclusion. This is at odds with the ratio of the Court of Appeal in *Greenhalgh* v *Arderne Cinemas Ltd* (4) in which Lord Evershed MR adopted the test of the hypothetical shareholder, ie to ask whether what was proposed was for that person's benefit. The test proposed in *Greenhalgh* (supra) is of little value where there is a conflict as in the instant case between two groups. Lord Evershed MR did however indicate that discriminatory conduct might be a ground for intervention. In the instant case it is not known exactly why Ox Ltd wishes to remove the pre-emption rights or exactly how it is intended to be beneficial to the company. Pin Ltd would therefore appear to be in a position to commence proceedings under s459 CA 1985 in order to seek redress.

The reduction of the preference dividend from 16 per cent to 10 per cent is undoubtedly a variation of the rights attaching to those shares: *House of Fraser Plc v AGCE Investments Ltd* (5); ie variation presupposes existence of the right, variation of the right, and the continued existence of the right. The resolution effecting the variation must therefore comply with any procedure laid down in the articles dealing with variation (if there is one): s125(4) CA 1985. If the articles do not provide any procedure for variation s125(2) provides a statutory procedure: this requires either a special majority of the holders of the class to consent in writing or an extraordinary resolution passed at a separate class meeting. The 15 per cent preference holders who object may apply to the court to have variation cancelled within 21 days of the consent/resolution being given/passed: s127(1) and (2). Where this mechanism is invoked the variation is of no effect unless approved by the court.

References

(1) [1987] Ch 1
(2) [1900] 1 Ch 656
(3) [1927] 2 KB 9
(4) [1951] Ch 286
(5) [1987] AC 387

QUESTION 8

General Comment

A fairly difficult question requiring the candidate to contemplate precisely the crux of the problem. Not to be undertaken without a very careful reading of and reflection upon the problem.

Skeleton Solution

Financial assistance – definition of – purpose of prohibition.

Fiduciary duties of directors – duty to act bona fide – duty not to act for any collateral purpose – principal and subsidiary purposes.

Suggested Solution

The directors of Tot Ltd must consider in depth two matters before purchasing the 'Biggerbyte 601'. In view of the fact that Ven intends to acquire further shares in Robber Plc the directors must question whether: (1) the purchase might fall foul of the financial assistance provisions in s151 CA 1985; and (2) whether in deciding whether or not to purchase the computer it is proper for them to have regard to Ven's proposed acquisition of shares in Robber Plc.

Dealing with the question of financial assistance, s151(1) CA 1985 prohibits the provision of financial assistance by a company or its subsidiary where a person is proposing to acquire shares in that company. On the facts Ven is quite clearly proposing to acquire shares in Robber Plc, the parent of Tot Ltd. The next step therefore is to ask whether there is financial assistance.

The principle underpinning the prohibition on financial assistance is to protect creditors from unlawful reductions of capital. Whilst financial assistance is defined very widely (but not exhaustively) in s152 of the Act it is worth bearing in mind the dictum of Hoffman J in *Charterhouse Investment Trust Ltd* v *Tempest Diesels Ltd* (1), that the prohibition is penal and ought not therefore to receive a strained construction in order to catch transactions not intended to be caught. This Hoffman J stated required the court to look at the 'realities' of the transaction. Assistance by gift or guarantee is usually fairly easy to recognise. What however where, as in the instant case, there is a straightforward purchase?

Financial assistance is defined in s152 CA 1985 as including the following: assistance by way of loan or any other agreement whereby the obligations of the giver are fulfilled at a time when reciprocal obligations remain unfulfilled. Also 'any other assistance' which reduces the assets of the company. This part of the definition arguably catches any transaction whereby the assistance is not matched by the company acquiring assets of an equivalent value. Applying this to the facts of the instant case it can be seen that Tot Ltd is to pay £180,000 for a computer which is arguably worth £250,000. The assets of Tot Ltd are likely therefore to be swelled rather than reduced and so the transaction does not reduce the company's assets. There is therefore no financial assistance within the meaning of the Act.

In committing Tot Ltd to the purchase, are the directors abusing their fiduciary duty to act in the best interests of the company? It is difficult to discern any consistent thread running through the authorities on this area. The predominance of authorities concern directors' improper allotments eg where at least one of the purposes of the allotment is to destroy an existing majority or to create a new one: *Hogg* v *Cramphorn Ltd* (2). The underlying principle is however the same. Can directors' actions be underpinned by a dual purpose or must directors never act for any collateral purpose?

In *Re Smith and Fawcett Ltd* (3), Lord Greene MR stated that directors should exercise their discretion in what they and not the court consider to be the best interests of the company, and not for any collateral purpose. The difficulty is of course that directors' actions are often motivated by any number of purposes. In *Mills* v *Mills* (4), Latham CJ stated that where there is more than one purpose, the proper question to be asked is, 'What is the moving cause?' Provided generally that the moving cause is the benefit of the company then the course of action will not be upset by the court.

This view was subsequently adopted by the Privy Council in *Howard Smith Ltd* v *Ampol Petroleum Ltd* (5). In particular Lord Wilberforce stated that the starting point would be to identify the power under consideration (eg, to allot shares) and then to examine the substantial purpose for which it was exercised. This approach seems at first glance very sensible. There may nevertheless be difficulties with it. It is presumably open to directors to attempt to protect themselves by passing a board resolution in favour of a particular course and to express as the dominant purpose what is in fact the subsidiary purpose. The courts will of course look at the factual reality of the situation as well as the declared intention of the directors. But the dominant purpose will be frequently difficult to ascertain. Once it is admitted that there is more than one purpose underpinning a particular act, how are the courts to determine dominancy? For example, as in the instant case, it may be that a new computer is very desirable (as is Ven's increased shareholding in Robber plc) rather than an absolute necessity.

It is useful to consider briefly the approach of the High Court of Australia in *Whitehouse* v *Carlton Pty Ltd* (6). In this case the court preferred to ask whether the exercise of a power was causally connected with collateral purpose ie if the power would not have been exercised 'but for the' collateral purpose then the exercise of that power should not be upheld. This approach arguably avoids the difficulties occasioned by the dominant purpose test but at the same time is a more stringent one. Applying the above to the facts of the problem it would be sensible to advise the directors of Tot Ltd to specifically direct their minds to the dominant purpose of the purchase and only if they conclude that they are principally motivated by benefit to Tot Ltd, to proceed with it.

References

(1) [1986] BCLC 1
(2) [1967] Ch 254
(3) [1942] Ch 304
(4) (1938) 60 CLR 150
(5) [1974] AC 821
(6) (1987) 11 ACLR 715